Much love,
Miss Toni

Four Seasons of Entertaining

Shayla Copas

Photography by Janet Warlick

Schiffer Publishing Ltd
4880 Lower Valley Road ■ Atglen, PA 19310

Recipes were provided by the culinary contributors in each chapter.

Photographs by Janet Warlick
Photographs on pages 4, 5, 27, the bottom of page 29, 30, 32, 33, 34, 35, 36, 37 by Erica Payne
Cover design by Ashlee Nobel
Page design by Ashlee Nobel
Type set in Sheila/Kepler Std/Adobe Garamond Pro

ISBN: 978-0-7643-5731-2
Printed in China

Published by Schiffer Publishing Ltd.
4880 Lower Valley Road
Atglen, PA 19310
Phone: (610) 593-1777; Fax. (610) 593-2002
E-mail: Info@schifferbooks.com
Web: www.schifferbooks.com

For our complete selection of fine books on this and related subjects please visit our website at www.schifferbooks.com You may also write for a free catalog.

Schiffer Publishing's titles are available at special discounts for bulk purchases for sales promotions or premiums. Special editions including personalized covers, corporate imprints, and excerpts, can be created in large quantities for special needs. For more information, contact the publisher.

We are always looking for people to write books on new and related subjects. If you have an idea for a new book, please contact us at proposals@schifferbooks.com.

This book is dedicated to the three most prominent mentors in my life.

To - My loving husband, Scott Copas (a.k.a. Scottkins), you are my heart, soul, and best friend. Thank you for being the rock of our family and for extending your strength and love to guide me throughout the last twenty-four years. I love you more than life itself and cannot imagine my world without you.

To - The most gracious hostess I've ever known, my mother-in-law, Sara Lay Copas, who is now hosting her celebrations in heaven. Sadly, due to a stroke, she could no longer entertain, but she continued her dream of hosting parties through me. Sara taught me the art of entertaining guests with style, grace, and love. I never host an important occasion without thinking of her or without the security of wearing her pearls for empowerment. I cannot think of a woman I admire more.

To - The Lord in Heaven, who is here through every season and who loves us unconditionally. I am grateful beyond words. Thank you for providing the strength, opportunities, and even the trials that have brought me to this moment. You have protected, guided, and inspired me.

Hebrews 13:2 – Do not neglect to show hospitality to strangers, for by this some have entertained angels without knowing it.

Acknowledgments

• • •

During my life and career, many people provided the knowledge, inspiration, and mentorship that made this book possible. Since this book's focus is on entertaining, however, I will acknowledge those who influenced my approach to entertaining and who were directly involved in the journey of this book.

I am eternally grateful for Janet Warlick, who spent countless hours shooting the exquisite photographs you see on these pages. She shared her talent and skills but also extended her friendship to me during the fifteen months we worked on this project. Janet has been a good friend and colleague for several years, but working together on this book has bonded us more deeply.

My husband, Scott Copas, is the consummate host, and I have learned so much from him. I'm originally from the North and his southern hospitality inspired me as we jointly hosted and chaired numerous balls, soirees, and events over the years. I am grateful for his spirit of embracing others and his love for being the life of the party.

I want to express my appreciation for my mother-in-law, Sara Lay Copas, who is now hosting her celebrations in heaven. She instilled in me her love of china, flatware, crystal, and stemware. I vividly remember the tears in her eyes when she bestowed upon me her beloved china before she passed.

I am thankful to Patricia McMillan, a friend and author with Schiffer Publishing who has taken an interest in my career and helped connect me with the publisher. I was blessed to be featured in Pat's book, *Christmas at Designers' Homes across America*, and am thankful for her support and mentorship throughout this process.

No event can be successful without a solid team, and I am most grateful for the floral designers, culinary experts, chefs, and others who added their expertise to this project: Dale Aldridge, Tammy Copeland, Brittany Vick, Angie Strange, Tanarah Haynie, Shay and Brian Geyer, Chef Jamie McAfee, Chef Tim Morton, Chef Janice Provost, Chef Payne Harding, Jim Norton, Chef Scott Rains, Chef Don Bingham, Chef Daniel Darrah, and First Lady Susan Hutchinson. I feel privileged and am overjoyed at the opportunity to display their talent throughout this book.

The names and websites of other key individuals involved can be found on the Resources and Credits page. I invite you to take the time to look through the list and familiarize yourself with them. I cannot begin to even express how much I appreciate the vendors, manufacturers, service providers, and creative talents who participated in this adventure. They were generous with the resources that made each event special and successful.

I am especially grateful for the inspiration and generosity of my dear friend Susan Hutchinson, who is the state's First Lady and who opens the Governor's Mansion (the "People's

House") to so many Arkansans and nonprofits each year. Her love of the state, its people, and the mansion is contagious as she dedicates herself to being a hospitable caretaker of the People's House. It is my honor to highlight the Governor's Mansion, a true treasure, so that all can enjoy its grandeur. This home has become quite special to me as I have been given the incredible opportunity to help design several areas of the mansion. Donating my design services to the Arkansas Governor's Mansion will be one of the fondest memories of my career. I remember the first time I witnessed a group of schoolchildren going through the mansion and saw their eyes light up as they passed by the mansion's treasures. At that moment, I realized that I was donating my time and talents to a cause that would be appreciated by generations to come.

While I'm speaking of the mansion and the First Lady, I also want to recognize the Arkansas Governor's Mansion Association, an incredible group of nonpartisan volunteers that raises the funds to keep the mansion beautiful. Our state is blessed to have this big-hearted group of people.

You'll no doubt be drawn to the textures and colors of the fabrics shown within these pages. For those, I'd like to applaud Callie Bullock of Draped and Tailored, who took on the enormous task of sewing each napkin and tablecloth that appears in almost every chapter of this book. Callie is a generous and talented spirit.

I want to thank all of the homeowners and guests who attended the parties described in this book. I have a couple of friends in particular I want to mention because I called on them on more occasions than I can count for support and to help gather dinner guests. I will be forever in debt to Sarah Hutchinson Wengel, who never failed to answer her phone when I called. I also want to recognize my dear friend, Aaron Perkins, for helping with that mission. The two of them were always available when I needed them; I am truly grateful for their loyalty and support.

I would be remiss if I didn't thank the talented people who worked on the editing, layout, food styling, and a few detail shots for the book. Rhonda Owen, Ashlee Nobel, Erica Payne, and Muriel Wilkins: thank you for being such an amazing team.

Last but not least, a huge thank-you to Pete Schiffer of Schiffer Publishing for believing in me, and to my editor, Cheryl Weber, for her guidance and patience.

With love and appreciation,

Shayla D. Copas

Shayla D. Copas

Introduction

· · ·

I adore every season of the year. Selecting a favorite would be like deciding on a favorite child or a favorite handbag. With the change of each season comes a sense of urgency to plan a party related to the time of year that's almost as strong as the "nesting" instinct of a new mom.

Entertaining has always been a part of my life, soul, and purpose. Nothing brings me more joy than to see the love on the faces of treasured friends as they converse and toast throughout the night. Something about a party makes life magical. And, of course, I always come off that high the next day as I'm scrubbing dishes in the kitchen.

After many years of hosting balls, soirees, and events with my dear husband, Scott, my career as a luxury interior designer has evolved to include the design and execution of many momentous occasions. However, those I remember most fondly are the themed seasonal parties. So, with those cherished memories, I decided to write a book about seasonal entertainment and the delicious cuisine that completes those occasions. Every event includes touches of the southern glam aesthetic that has become my trademark.

I clearly remember the first party I planned, because it was my own wedding reception. We didn't have a lot of money at the time and my budget was tight. I am so thankful to have had that experience, because it taught me to be inventive and use my creativity. This has helped me time after time to come up with approachable ideas for events. While the presentations in this book are elegant, they are also grounded with ideas that won't deplete your pocketbook. On the other hand, some chapters feature over-the-top tablescapes and tips that will get your creativity flowing on a different level.

This book includes four themed parties per season to inspire you as you create your own soirees. The events were held in Arkansas, Tennessee, and Texas. I planned, designed, and executed all sixteen parties in a fifteen-month period and had the time of my life while doing it. I will never forget being on the road with my dear friend and photographer, Janet Warlick. We created many hilarious memories to be cherished and enjoyed many a glass of wine toasting each event as we wrapped up the shoots.

From the Oakmont Estate in Tennessee to the Arkansas Governor's Mansion, you will find the venues gorgeous and diverse. The chefs and a sampling of their recipes from each event will charm even the most discriminating foodie. From elementary to advanced, there is something for everyone. And in the Kentucky Derby section, I have even tucked in a few of my favorite recipes. I enjoy cooking almost as much as planning the party.

So, grab a glass of wine and savor the moment as you begin to plan your own memorable occasions. Cheers!

Contents

• • •

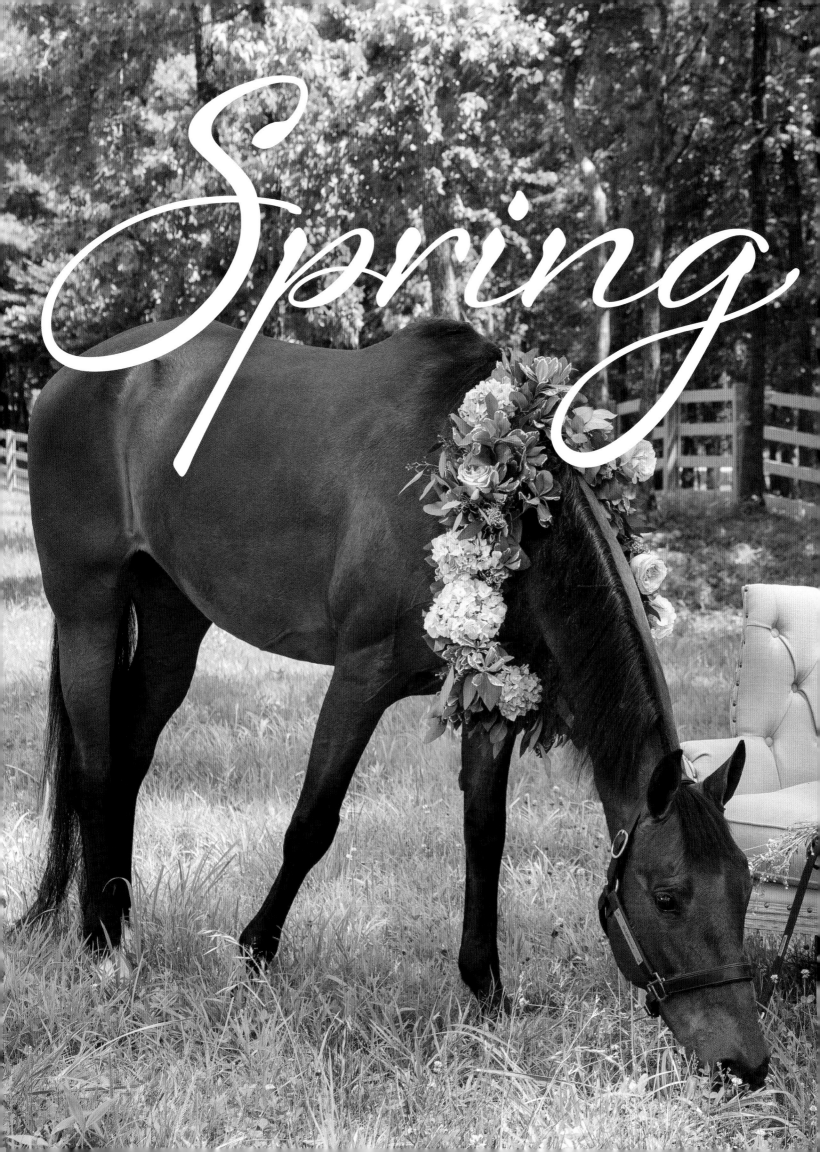

Spring

Kentucky Derby
Luncheon at the Stable

Rich in tradition and history, the Kentucky Derby, a.k.a. "The Run for the Roses," is the longest-running sporting event in US history. Each year on the first Saturday in May, men in seersucker suits and bow ties and women in fascinators or elaborate designer hats line the stands to cheer for their favorite ponies. After attending the event with my design family, I returned home inspired to throw my own Derby-themed soiree. I knew the perfect place in Arkansas for a Kentucky Derby luncheon— the Pine Hill Ranch, a world-class, newly built equestrian center in Little Rock.

The 250-acre Pine Hill Ranch is majestic and breathtaking. Home to Red Hot Momma, a retired world champion show horse, it consists of a lodge, equestrian center, and show barn that would impress even the most seasoned equestrian. The Pine Hill Ranch was the dream of Little Rock resident Bob Mullenax, who has been keenly interested in horses since he was a child. In 2004, he purchased Red Hot Momma for a mere $1,000. The show horse then went on to win six world championships before Mullenax retired her in 2015.

TIP

Find a venue that suits the theme. A stable or equestrian center is an ideal setting for a Kentucky Derby–focused luncheon. Find a way to include horses, and you've created not only an event but a memorable experience.

"*Behind every legend lies
an impossible dream.*"

Southern Tradition

I wanted the table setting to be feminine and elegant. Pearls, roses, and crystal are just a few luxurious items that remind me of southern tradition. Kim Seybert silver chargers adorned with pearls complemented the Kate Spade Larabee Road Platinum dinnerware. Napkins, made with Thibaut's Anna French Villeneuve pattern in a soft dusty rose, were laid gracefully over each plate. Nachtmann's symmetrical cut stemware bestowed an air of contemporary elegance and refinement. It's fun to mix formality with rustic elements in a casual space.

Run for the Roses

Roses are synonymous with the Kentucky Derby, and I wanted to include them. However, I did not want to use the traditional red rose. Silks A Bloom designed lush floral arrangements of Quicksand, pink Mondale, and White Polar Star roses mixed with hydrangeas, pink rice flowers, white anemones, dusty miller, white snapdragons, and white French tulips. We used Park Hill Collection's Grand Champion Silver Cups for vases.

TIP

Creative elements bring the look together. Try using driftwood as the foundation for floral on a table. Or embellish a Derby hat with fresh floral for the hors d'oeuvres table.

• • •

Millionaires Row

If I'm hosting an outdoor event, I use furniture to soften the space and add to the ambience. For a Derby luncheon, a bar is a must, so we incorporated Park Hill's Vintage Counter Bar. Our neighbor, Herren Hickingbotham, is a part owner of Park Hill Collection, a furnishings and accessories company known for rustic elegance. I chose them for this setting because they provide an authentic, detailed look and have a vast product line. Storage in the back of the bar gave us space to tuck away our wine, extra dinnerware, and glasses.

Because I'm almost always in party-planning mode, when I purchase new furniture for our home I look for pieces that can serve double duty. Will it work for the space and will it function as a prop for a future event? I find that I get more use from my purchases if I shop with a multi-use frame of mind.

Derby Soirée

Pimento Cheese and Ham
Tea Sandwiches

Derby Chicken Salad
on Apple Slices topped
with Walnuts

Baked Brie with Bourbon
Candied Pecans and Rosemary

Mini Caprese Basil Salad Bites

Strawberry Mango Salsa
in Filo Cups

Pink Lemonade Rosé Fizz

Kentucky Derby Recipes
Courtesy of Shayla Copas

PIMENTO CHEESE AND HAM TEA SANDWICHES

Serves 12

12 slices honey ham

12 slices bread

16 ounces extra-sharp cheddar cheese

8 ounces of cream cheese, softened

½ cup mayonnaise

4 ounces chopped pimentos

½ teaspoon garlic powder

½ teaspoon dried onion flakes

¼ teaspoon salt

¼ teaspoon pepper

Pint of cherry tomatoes for garnish

Combine all ingredients except the ham and the bread in a mixing bowl. Mix with an electric mixer on low and increase speed over a minute's time until all ingredients are combined. Place in an airtight container and refrigerate for 2 hours. Line up 6 slices of bread and top each with two slices of ham, then spread with ¼ cup of pimento cheese. Top each sandwich with another piece of bread. Refrigerate for an hour until chilled and pimento cheese firms. Trim crust and cut each large sandwich into four fingers with a serrated knife. Slice the cherry tomatoes in half and place atop the sandwiches.

CHICKEN SALAD ON APPLE SLICES TOPPED WITH WALNUTS

Serves 12

1 package frozen chicken breasts

2 tablespoons tub-style cream cheese, softened

9 heaping tablespoons mayonnaise

1 teaspoon apple cider vinegar

¼ teaspoon white pepper

¾ cup chopped celery

1 cup green seedless grapes, sliced in half

2 tablespoons sweet relish

1 cup dried cranberries

Pink Himalayan sea salt to taste

6 medium apples cored and sliced

1½ cups large walnuts

Directions

Cook chicken breasts and shred with a fork. Combine cream cheese, mayonnaise, vinegar, and pepper in a medium bowl. Stir in shredded chicken breasts, celery, grapes, relish, and dried cranberries. Salt to taste. Spread on apple slices and garnish each slice with a walnut.

BAKED BRIE WITH BOURBON CANDIED PECANS

Serves 12

1 6–8-ounce wheel of brie

½ cup chopped pecans

2 tablespoons dark brown sugar

1 tablespoon butter

Dash salt

3 tablespoons real maple syrup

2 tablespoons brandy or bourbon

Rosemary for garnish

½ cup additional pecans for garnish

Gluten-free crackers for serving

Preheat oven to 350 degrees. If you choose, slice the top of the rind off the brie. Place the cheese cut side up on a cookie sheet and bake about 15 minutes. When there is about 5 minutes left of baking time, make the pecan topping.

Pecan topping: Heat a dry skillet over medium-high heat. Add pecans and toast them 1–2 minutes, stirring frequently. Add brown sugar, butter, salt, maple syrup, and bourbon. Stir to combine and continue to cook until sugar has dissolved and pecans are coated evenly with some syrup remaining. Remove cheese from oven and transfer to a serving plate. Pour the pecan mixture evenly over the top of the cheese and garnish with rosemary and a few additional pecans, if available. Serve with gluten-free crackers.

MINI CAPRESE BITES

Serves 12

¼ cup extra-virgin olive oil

2 tablespoons balsamic vinegar

¼ teaspoon kosher salt

¼ teaspoon pepper

½ pound fresh mozzarella

Fresh basil leaves

1 pint cherry tomatoes

Combine oil, vinegar, salt, and pepper in small bowl. Cut the mozzarella into cubes. Place on a plate in a single layer and drizzle with the oil-and-vinegar mixture. Cut the tomatoes in halves. Place a basil leaf onto a toothpick, then a tomato slice, a piece of cheese, and another tomato slice. The tomato bottom should be facing down on the toothpick. Drizzle with oil and vinegar mixture.

STRAWBERRY MANGO SALSA IN PHYLLO CUPS

Serves 12

2 cups fresh strawberries, diced

2 small mangoes, diced

2 small avocados, diced

1 jalapeño, diced

1 cup fresh cilantro, chopped

¼ cup lime juice

24 phyllo cups

Combine all ingredients in a large bowl. Place a spoonful in each phyllo cup and garnish with a sprig of cilantro.

PINK LEMONADE ROSÉ FIZZ

Per serving

1 tablespoon pink lemonade concentrate, per serving

Rosé

Club soda

Light pink cookie sugar

½ cup lemon juice

Fresh lemons for garnish

Lemon or edible flowers for garnish

Place pink lemonade concentrate in a glass. Fill the glass two-thirds with rosé. Fill it with about ¼ cup of club soda or to taste. Stir in a splash of lemon juice. Stir well and add ice. Spread a large amount of the cookie sugar on a small plate. Place ½ cup of lemon juice in a small bowl. Place the rim of the cup in the lemon juice and then roll in the sugar to coat the rim. Pour lemonade mixture in the sugar-coated glass, then garnish with lemon wedges and edible flowers.

Spring Rehearsal Dinner
Farm-to-Table Elegance

I am enchanted by the sights and smells of spring. Flowers blooming, fanciful airborne fragrances, birds chirping—life just seems new. Of every event in the book, this is the closest to my heart. My stepson, a child who has been like my own since he was nine years old, was getting married, and I had the honor of planning his rehearsal dinner. Nick was the child I talked to almost daily, so every detail about his rehearsal dinner was close to my heart. He had asked me not only to plan the dinner, but also to serve as the ordained minister for his wedding. So I was the stepmother of the groom, in charge of a dinner for ninety guests, and preparing to perform my first wedding as an ordained minister.

Nick's fiancé, Ann, has classic taste with an air of simplicity, so I decided to go with a refined farm-to-table theme. I rented rustic but elegant farm-to-table furnishings to create the ambiance for our dinner. The yin to the yang was the fine china and crystal contrasting with, yet complementing, the wood grain of the furnishings. Charles Sadek's Exotic Bird china pattern paired exquisitely with the upscale country theme. I enlisted Chef Tim Morton of RH Catering for the evening. He prepared a four-course menu featuring fresh, local ingredients.

TIP

Don't be afraid to mix rustic and classic design elements. Crystal, fine china, and wood grain married well with our theme. Monogrammed hemstitched ecru napkins were folded uniformly under the plates and sported the letter "C" embroidered in gold.

· · ·

Fanciful Florals

The newly renovated farmhouse owned by Linda
and Rush Harding had lofty ceilings that allowed
us to go tall with our arrangements. Centerpieces soared above the guests to create a canopy of
florals. We placed succulents, gold-gilded pears,
fresh moss, and grapes down the center of the
tables to create the illusion of a runner. Midsized
arrangements in varying heights were filled with
fresh tulips, roses, and hydrangeas.

Sweet Sentiment

Sentimental, heartfelt touches impact an event in special ways. I decided to give each woman at our rehearsal dinner a three-part gift. Their lavishly wrapped boxes included a handkerchief for the wedding ceremony, a note hand-written exclusively for each attendee, and a poem on heavy card stock. The poem read, "May you have tears of joy, tears of laughter, tears of happily ever after."

TIP

I don't know how many times I've broken a cherished piece of china, only to find out that it's out of production. A hidden gem that a lot of party enthusiasts have yet to discover is Replacements Ltd., the world's largest supplier of vintage and current dinnerware. They also carry crystal, silver, and collectibles. So next time you drop your great-grandmother's plate, remember that they are just a phone call away.

TIP

Try layering textured card stock when creating menus for your next soiree. We designed unique menus for each event in this book with the help of By Invitation Only in Little Rock, Arkansas. The back layer of our Spring Rehearsal Dinner menu had a wood grain texture that coordinated with our farm-to-table theme. Menu cards not only add a personal touch but also allow guests to scan the food offerings for potential allergies.

Personal Touches

Guests listened intently as we went around the room toasting the bride and groom after the lavish dinner. Guests also viewed a video with photos of the bride and groom that I spent months compiling. There wasn't a dry eye in the room and the handkerchiefs came in quite handy. The video soundtrack included songs that had special meaning or relevance to the couple, which helped set the mood.

TIP

Handwritten notes to each attendee with a sentimental gift can bond a group as they compare their notes. A personalized video with photos from childhood adds laughter and tears of joy to the evening.

TIP

When speeches are given at a large rehearsal dinner, an audio system is a must. Because our dinner was located in three rooms, we also included screens so that all of our guests could enjoy the video. Speakers throughout the space allowed all to be part of the festivities no matter where they were located.

THE REHEARSAL DINNER
HONORING

Ann Gunti & Nick Copas

FRIDAY, APRIL 21, 2017 · 7:30 P.M.
HARDING FARM

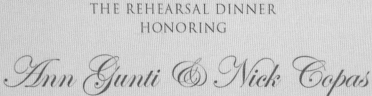

First Course

COMPRESSED ARKANSAS HEIRLOOM TOMATO SALAD

FRESH GULF SHRIMP, CRISPY ARKANSAS FRIED OKRA,
MICRO GREENS, SHERRY VINAIGRETTE

WINE PAIRING - EDNA VALLEY CHARDONNAY

ORGANIC KIWI SORBET

Main Course

SMOKED PRIME STONECREEK FILET

LUMP CRAB AND CORN STUFFED VIDALIA ONION,
SMOKED PETIT JEAN BACON WRAPPED
GREEN BEAN BUNDLES, CACHE STEAK SAU

WINE PAIRING - TAKEN R

Dessert Cours

PAN FRIED POUND

HOMEMADE VANIL
MACERATED PEACH, LEMON C

WINE PAIRING - LE TERTRE DU LYS D'OR

Meal is entirely gluten free

Spring Rehearsal Dinner Recipes

Courtesy of Chef Tim Morton, RH Catering

FRESH GULF SHRIMP ON HEIRLOOM TOMATO SALAD TOPPED WITH FRIED OKRA, MICROGREENS, AND SHERRY VINAIGRETTE

Serves 8

Heirloom Tomato Salad

3 heirloom tomatoes

Extra-virgin olive oil

Sprig of thyme

Salt and pepper to taste

Directions

Slice tomatoes ¼ inch thick. Season with salt, pepper, olive oil, and thyme. Seal in a plastic bag and refrigerate 24 hours before serving. Served as the foundation to the Fresh Gulf Shrimp.

Fresh Gulf Shrimp and Crispy Arkansas Fried Okra

Per serving

3 fresh Gulf shrimp

Blackened seasoning

8 okra

Buttermilk

Cornmeal

Salt and pepper to taste

Olive oil

Microgreens for garnish

Directions

Peel and devein shrimp; season with blackening spice and place in the refrigerator. Trim off okra ends and soak 30 minutes in buttermilk. In a bowl, mix cornmeal, salt, and pepper. Heat 1 tablespoon olive oil in a pan. Dredge okra in seasoned cornmeal and fry in olive oil until crispy. Grill shrimp. Serve shrimp atop the heirloom tomato salad with fried okra, microgreens, and vinaigrette drizzled on top.

Sherry Vinaigrette

Serves 8

3 cloves minced roasted garlic

1 tablespoon Dijon

2 tablespoon honey

1 cup sherry vinegar

1 tablespoon chopped fresh thyme

½ cup olive oil

Directions

Combine all ingredients in mixing bowl and whisk together, adding oil last, slowly. The custom vinaigrette and microgreens complement the prime offerings of the South—blackened shrimp and okra—for a flavor sensation like no other.

SMOKED PRIME STONECREEK FILET WITH CACHE STEAK SAUCE

Per serving

7-ounce center-cut filet

Petit Jean bacon

Salt and pepper to taste

Wrap steak in Petit Jean bacon. Season with salt and pepper. Grill to desired temperature and serve immediately. The center-cut filet accented by the Petit Jean bacon has no need for further flavoring due to the top-quality ingredients expertly prepared. Serve immediately topped with cache sauce.

Cache Steak Sauce

Serves 4

1 cup Worcestershire

1 cup demi-glace

1 tablespoon horseradish

2 tablespoon butter

In a saucepan reduce Worcestershire, demi-glace, and horseradish by half. Stir in butter. Strain and serve.

LUMP CRAB AND CORN–STUFFED VIDALIA ONION

Serves 8

4 Vidalia onions

4 tablespoons olive oil

1 cup panko bread crumbs (reserve a few for broiling at the end)

1 teaspoon Himalayan sea salt

1 teaspoon white pepper

2 ears corn, shucked, boiled 5 minutes, and corn cut off

1 cup mascarpone, softened

½ cup cream cheese, softened

3 egg yolks, beaten

1 tablespoon thyme

1 pound lump crab

Peel and halve onions. Place in a baking pan and drizzle each onion with a tablespoon of olive oil. Cover the pan with foil and roast in a 400-degree oven for 45 minutes. Remove from oven and chill. Remove inner rings, leaving a ½-inch-thick cup. Mix bread crumbs (except the portion reserved for broiling), salt, and pepper in bowl. Mix remaining ingredients except crab until smooth. Fold in crab and pipe the mixture into onions. Bake on a lightly greased sheet pan at 375 degrees for 30 minutes. Top with remaining bread crumb mixture and broil for the last few minutes. Watch closely. Season with salt and pepper.

SMOKED PETIT JEAN BACON–WRAPPED GREEN BEAN BUNDLES

2 pounds whole fresh green beans, blanched

1 slab Smoked Petit Jean bacon, lightly cooked

Wrap bundles of 3–4 green beans in bacon strips. Place in a greased baking pan and bake at 375 degrees for 30 minutes. Salt and pepper to taste.

GLUTEN-FREE PAN-FRIED SOUR CREAM POUND CAKE WITH MACERATED PEACHES AND LEMON CHANTILLY CREAM

Serves 6

Sour Cream Pound Cake

2 sticks unsalted butter, room temperature, plus more for frying

3 cups sugar

6 eggs, room temperature

1 teaspoon gluten-free vanilla extract

¼ teaspoon salt

3 cups gluten-free flour

½ teaspoon baking soda

1 cup sour cream, room temperature

Directions

Preheat oven to 325 degrees. Coat tube pan with cooking spray or butter. In a stand mixer, cream together the butter and sugar for 3 to 5 minutes. Add eggs one at a time, beating well after each one. Add vanilla and salt. Stir together flour and baking soda, then add dry ingredients to wet ingredients just until half-mixed. Add sour cream. Mix until all ingredients are combined and batter looks creamy, but don't overmix. Pour into prepared tube pan and bake on the center rack about 90 minutes until a cake tester comes out clean.

When the cake is done, cooled, and sliced, place a 12-inch sauté pan over medium heat. Butter each side of the pound cake slices with 1½ teaspoons of butter. Sauté for a minute per side. Remove each cake slice to a plate.

Macerated Peaches

8 ripe fresh peaches, halved and sliced

1 cup light brown sugar

1 cup sugar

Pinch of salt

⅛ teaspoon nutmeg

⅛ teaspoon cinnamon

1 teaspoon ground cloves

Directions

Peel peaches and cut in half, then slice and set aside. In a mixing bowl mix the sugars, salt, nutmeg, cinnamon, and ground clove. Toss mixture with peaches in a vacuum-sealed bag or zippered bag. Compress and chill three hours, remove the bag from the refrigerator, and let set at room temperature until ready to serve. Spoon peach mixture over the cake and finish with Lemon Chantilly Cream. Accompany with vanilla ice cream and a sprig of mint.

Lemon Chantilly Cream

3 cups heavy cream

Zest of 1 lemon

8 egg yolks

3 cups powdered sugar

1½ cup Grand Marnier

Directions

Whip heavy cream and lemon zest in a bowl until soft peaks form. Set aside. In a mixer fitted with a whip attachment, beat egg yolks until they triple in size. Gradually add powdered sugar and Grand Marnier. Fold in heavy cream mixture and chill until ready to serve.

Easter
Brunch at the Governor's Mansion

I can't think of a better place to enjoy Easter brunch than at the Arkansas Governor's Mansion. Fondly known as the "People's House," the house and its residents have a special place in my heart. I was given the amazing opportunity of designing several of its interior spaces over the last few years. The facelift, all done with First Lady Susan Hutchinson's impeccable attention to detail, was tedious at times but well worth the hard work. The Governor's Mansion opened its doors in 1950 and has since been the home of eleven governors.

When designing an event in a home as significant as this one, it's important to keep the elements of the room in mind when selecting linens, decor, and floral. The antique Persian rug donated by Governor Winthrop Rockefeller and the wallcovering our team helped to design inspired the tablescape design. I incorporated orange, coral, and light spring colors that would complement the room's foundation.

TIP

When designing an event in a historic room, work within its existing feel and color framework.

An Abundant Garden

I added spring touches to the Easter table with bird's nests, eggs, rabbits, and an abundance of fresh produce. Tanarah Haynie, lead floral designer with Tanarah Luxe Floral, incorporated a glorious combination of long-stemmed Redwood Grove French tulips en masse with garden produce for a delightfully original display.

TIP

Use sentimental or significant household treasures as floral containers. The Governor's Mansion silver from the battleship USS Arkansas *proudly holds an Easter floral arrangement containing French tulips and fresh carrots.*

FUN FACT

For our stemware, I used the mansion's Waterford crystal, which has graced many a dinner or luncheon for dignitaries from across the world. The striking pattern is called Araglin. Concrete bunnies holding fresh carrots add a touch of whimsy to the elegant tablescape.

◆ ◆ ◆

I adore the mansion's Lenox Springfield pattern that was modified with the Arkansas State Seal. Sublimely elegant, it served as a beautiful canvas for our spring bird nests. The mansion's antique Gorham Silver in the Melrose pattern provided a bit of historical detail to the table and went perfectly with our linens constructed of Thibaut's Jakarata pattern.

"Spring translates Earth's happiness into colorful flowers."
—*Terri Guillemets*

• • •

To Design a Mockingbird

The design of the hand-painted silk wall covering by Paul Montgomery came to fruition through an immense amount of patience and creativity. My firm, along with First Lady Susan Hutchinson, took an existing pattern and added Arkansas birds, which included the mockingbird, and indigenous florals. Mrs. Hutchinson weighed in heavily on the scale of the birds and floral when creating the design. Her in-depth knowledge of feathered creatures made this project educational and fun. We had numerous strikeoffs with the manufacturers to get the mockingbird perfect for production. This wall covering in the mansion Dining Room served as a perfect spring backdrop for the Easter brunch.

SALADS
Easter Basket Salad
Spinach and Mushroom Salad

ENTRÉE
Tarragon Chicken
served with
Easter Egg Bread

DESSERT
Lemon Roll with Strawberries
and Lemon Filling

Easter Brunch Recipes

Courtesy of Chef Don Bingham Retired administrator of the Arkansas Governor's Mansion

CHICKEN BREASTS TARRAGON WITH SHERRY PAN GRAVY

Serves 4

4 whole chicken breasts (about 1 pound each)

2 tablespoons salad or olive oil

2 tablespoons butter or margarine

6 shallots, chopped

2 pared carrots, sliced into ¼-inch rounds

¼ cup cognac or brandy

1 cup dry white wine

¼ cup chopped fresh tarragon

½ teaspoon chervil or parsley leaves

1 teaspoon salt

⅛ teaspoon pepper

1 cup light cream

1 egg yolk

1 tablespoon all-purpose flour

½ pound mushrooms, washed and thinly sliced

2 tablespoons butter or margarine

Sprigs of fresh tarragon

Directions

In a 6-quart Dutch oven, heat oil and 2 tablespoons butter. Add chicken breasts (half at a time, enough to cover bottom of the pan); sauté, turning on all sides, until brown. Remove chicken as it browns. To drippings in Dutch oven, add shallots and carrots; sauté, stirring, 5 minutes or until golden brown. Return chicken to Dutch oven, and heat. Slightly heat cognac in ladle and ignite. Add white wine, tarragon, chervil, salt, and pepper. Bring to a boil, reduce heat, and simmer gently, covered, for 30 minutes. Remove chicken to heated serving platter; keep warm.

Strain drippings and vegetables from Dutch oven and return sauce to Dutch oven. In small bowl, combine cream, egg yolk, and flour; mix well with wire whisk. Stir the cream sauce into the Dutch oven and bring

just to boiling, stirring. Add more wine if sauce seems too thick. Meanwhile, sauté mushrooms in hot butter 5 minutes, until tender. Spoon sauce over chicken. Garnish with tarragon and mushrooms.

EASTER BASKET SALAD WITH AVOCADO

Serves 6

8 hard-boiled eggs, shelled

Pastel food coloring

1 large head Boston lettuce

¼ small head chicory

2 small avocados

1 small tomato

¼ cup mayonnaise

¼ cup sour cream

2 teaspoons grated or dried onion

1 teaspoon salt

2 tablespoons lemon juice

Fill several small, deep cups with water. Stir a few drops food coloring into each to tint pink, green, yellow, orange, or other colors of your choice. Place 1 egg into each cup; let stand, turning several times, until delicately tinted. Remove from water; drain on paper towel. Repeat with remaining eggs; chill. Wash lettuce and chicory; dry well. Separate leaves; chill.

Cut, pit, and peel avocados and mash well in a small bowl. Dice tomato and stir into avocado with mayonnaise, sour cream, onion, salt, and lemon juice; chill. Just

before serving, line a large salad bowl with small lettuce leaves; break remaining leaves into bite-sized pieces and place in bowl; top with chicory. Nestle eggs in greens. Pass dressing separately.

LEMON ROLL WITH STRAWBERRIES

Serves 6

3 eggs

1 cup granulated sugar

⅓ cup water

1 teaspoon vanilla

¾ cup all-purpose flour

1 teaspoon baking powder

¼ teaspoon salt

½ cup powdered sugar

2 pints strawberries

¼ cup granulated sugar

3 kiwi fruit, sliced for garnish

Mint leaves for garnish

Heat oven to 375 degrees. Line jelly roll pan with aluminum foil or waxed paper; grease generously. Beat eggs in small bowl on high speed until thick and lemon-colored, about 5 minutes. Pour eggs into large bowl. Beat in 1 cup granulated sugar gradually; add water and vanilla on low speed. Add flour, baking powder, and salt gradually, beating until batter is smooth. Pour into pan, spreading batter to corners. Bake 12–15 minutes.

Immediately loosen cake from edge of pan; invert on towel sprinkled with powdered sugar. Carefully remove foil; trim off stiff edges of cake. Roll hot cake and towel from narrow end and cool. Prepare Clear Lemon Filling and cool. Unroll cake, remove towel, and spread cake with filling. Roll up and refrigerate no longer than 24 hours.

Reserve 8 medium strawberries; slice remaining strawberries. Sprinkle sliced strawberries with ¼ cup granulated sugar. Garnish with reserved strawberries, kiwi slices, and mint leaves. Serve sliced strawberries with roll.

Clear Lemon Filling

¾ cup granulated sugar

3 tablespoons cornstarch

¼ teaspoon salt

¾ cup water

1 tablespoon margarine or butter

1 teaspoon grated lemon peel

⅓ cup lemon juice

4 drops yellow food coloring, optional

Mix sugar, cornstarch, and salt in saucepan. Stir in water gradually. Cook, stirring constantly, until mixture thickens. Boil and stir 1 minute; remove from heat. Stir in margarine and lemon peel. Stir in lemon juice gradually and, if desired, 4 drops yellow food coloring. If filling is too soft, refrigerate until set.

Cinco de Mayo
A Festive Celebration

OK, I'll admit it, Cinco de Mayo is my favorite chapter of this book. The home of Susan and Herren Hickingbotham was the ideal festive venue for our celebration. I love color—and the bolder the better—so I specified a fun mixture of Thibaut fabrics for our napkins and tablecloths. A marriage of hot pink, orange, and cream flows throughout this Cinco de Mayo tablescape to provide a festive feeling.

You can use residential fabrics for table linens as long as you treat them with a stain repellant before use. The repellant will help spilled liquids bead instead of soaking into the tablecloth. I spray mine with MicroSeal. The use of residential textiles for table linens opens up an entire world of possibilities for event design. You can find gorgeous textiles and have your seamstress create the linens. I teamed up with Callie Bullock of Draped and Tailored, who did a phenomenal job constructing the linens for Cinco de Mayo and other chapters of this book. She paid close attention to detail, which is important when selecting a workroom to sew your linens.

TIP

For Cinco de Mayo, make a splash with bright and cheerful textiles. A mixture of Thibaut fabrics in bright colors were a hit. I chose the Sunburst pattern for the tablecloth in the color combination pink/coral; for the napkin, Thibaut's Wavelet pattern coordinated perfectly.

Olé!

With hot pink, orange, and cream as my primary palette, I needed a metal tone to accent the table. Gold worked perfectly with our color combo, so I selected Kim Seybert's Sahara chargers to ground the cream Skyros Cantaria dinnerware. I love Skyros because its products are safe for the oven, freezer, microwave, and dishwasher. They also don't chip easily, which works well for this klutzy cook.

Thank goodness, I wasn't in the kitchen that day. I called on my friend Chef Scott Rains from Table 28 in Little Rock, Arkansas, to prepare his favorite Cinco de Mayo specialties. His recipes are featured at the end of this chapter.

TIP

Stemware is often the jewelry of the table. For Cinco de Mayo, try stemware with a touch of gold. I selected Kim Seybert's Helix collection because of its ombre gold finish. Gold flatware from Mepra completes the look.

FUN FACT

Did you know that Cinco de Mayo is sometimes confused with Mexico's Independence Day, which is actually September 16? In the United States, the day has become a celebration of Mexican American culture; in Mexico, Cinco de Mayo still commemorates a historic battle.

A Floral Fantasy

A mixture of poppy pods, pink hydrangeas, Pink Floyd roses, Bells of Ireland, yellow billy buttons, and other floral varieties graced the table. Floral designers Dale Aldridge, Tammy Copeland, and Brittany Vick of Silks A Bloom in Little Rock, Arkansas, provided the floral design and knocked it out of the park. Mixing in a few colors outside of your palette provides depth and harmony. Here, yellow and green in the floral compositions created that effect.

An arrangement brimming with floral and tropical greenery added an elegant touch to the pool.

Lights strung in the backyard provided ambience and extra flare, while an arrangement cascading down the fountain drew the eye to a key focal for our event.

Find Your Place

I always love to find unusual items to serve as place cards, which you will see displayed throughout this book. For Cinco de Mayo, I specified Xela Aroma's gorgeous Metallic Ombre mercury glass candles because of the agate accent on the lid. I had By Invitation Only in Little Rock add the names of my guests in gold metallic ink to personalize the table. Place cards give guests a sense of inclusion as well as letting them know where the host wants them to sit. I don't know how many parties I've attended where we seemed to play musical chairs because guests were unsure of the order. Place cards solve this uncomfortable issue and make everyone feel welcome.

"Tell me who your friends are and I'll tell you who you are."
—Mexican Proverb

Cinco de Mayo Recipes

Courtesy of Chef Scott Rains, Table 28

TEQUILA ME SOFTLY MARGARITA

Serves 1

⅛ teaspoon brown sugar

⅛ teaspoon water

⅛ teaspoon cinnamon

1 ounce pineapple juice

2 ounces tequila blanco

¾ ounce dry curaçao

¼ ounce agave

1 ounce lime juice

Pineapple slices for garnish

Directions

Dissolve brown sugar in water. Add cinnamon and pineapple juice. Fill shaker cup with ice. Add all ingredients, including the brown sugar and cinnamon mixture. Shake, then pour over strainer into glass and garnish with a pineapple slice.

TRES LECHES BREAD PUDDING

Serves 6

1 pound bolillo (bread)

1 can evaporated milk

1 can sweetened condensed milk

¾ cup heavy cream

2 teaspoons vanilla

1 teaspoon cinnamon

1 teaspoon nutmeg

6 whole eggs

1 cup of sugar

1 can cajeta (Mexican caramel sauce)

Cherries for garnish

Directions

Preheat oven to 350 degrees. Liberally spray or butter baking dish or dishes until coated. Combine cubed bolillo, evaporated milk, sweet milk, heavy cream, vanilla, cinnamon, and nutmeg. Let soak a minimum of an hour, or overnight for better results. Mix eggs and sugar together. Fold into bread mixture. Ladle or spoon into baking dish. Bake 30–40 minutes until firm in the middle.

Icing

1 pint heavy cream

4 tablespoons sugar

Directions

Beat heavy cream in a mixing bowl with whip attachment. Add sugar and continue whipping until stiff peaks form. Spoon or pipe whipped cream icing on bread pudding, drizzle with cajeta, and garnish with cherries.

CHARRED PULPO APPETIZER

1 whole pulpo (octopus)

2 lemons, divided

11 quarts bouillon liquid (see instructions)

1½ cups white dry wine

Salt (pinch)

1 cup olive oil, plus more for drizzling

Dry seasoning (see recipe)

Juice one lemon and reserve the two halves. Cover octopus with bouillon (water, wine, lemon and juice, and salt) in a stock pot. Add a heavy plate or pan to weigh the octopus down, submerging it in the liquid. Simmer octopus for 1½–2 hours until tender. Cool and then portion by separating legs with a knife. Discard eyes and beak. Drizzle octopus with olive oil, coat with dry seasoning, and sear in a cast-iron or charcoal grill until blackened on all sides. Serve with Cilantro Aioli and wedges from the second lemon.

Dry seasoning

2 tablespoons paprika

1 tablespoon black pepper

Chili flakes to taste

1 teaspoon oregano

1 teaspoon lemon peel

Mix all ingredients together.

CILANTRO AIOLI

2 egg yolks

2 teaspoons mustard

3 tablespoons mayonnaise

3 teaspoons lime juice

2 tablespoons chopped cilantro

Salt

½ cup olive oil

Add yolks to mustard, mayo, lime juice, cilantro, and a liberal amount of salt in a food processor. While processor is running slowly, add oil in a steady stream.

TOSTADAS DE CARNITAS DE PATO WITH FOIE GRAS CREMA

1 whole duckling
Olive oil
12 whole peppercorns
1 orange (peel only)
6 sprigs fresh cilantro, minced
6 sprigs fresh thyme
1 whole garlic in pod (crushed and broken in husk)
Salt to taste
Corn tortillas
Desired toppings
Foie Gras Crema

Heat oven to 250 degrees. Place duck in a baking dish. Cover the duck in oil and add all the dry ingredients. Roast 4–6 hours. While meat is still warm, remove the meat from the bone and shred or chop. Fry corn tortillas in pan with oil and place on a paper towel. To plate, place duck and desired topping on corn tortillas. Drizzle with Foie Gras Crema.

Tip: Save the duck confit (fat). You can fry potatoes in it or use it as shortening for biscuits or a savory pie crust.

Foie Gras Crema

1 cup heavy cream
1 tablespoon buttermilk
Juice of half a lime
Pinch of salt
2–4 ounces foie gras (cooked and diced)

Mix the heavy cream, buttermilk, lime juice, and salt. Cover with plastic wrap or store in a jar with lid. Leave it out overnight to begin the culturing process. In the morning, it should be smooth and thick like crème fraiche or slightly runny sour cream. Sear the pieces of foie gras (if you can't find foie gras, leave it out, since the recipe will be delicious without it). Cool, then stir into the crema along with the fat that has seeped out (that is the good part). Serve immediately or chill. Lasts up to a week in the refrigerator.

Summer

Seersucker Social
A Garden-Inspired Party

When evenings grow warmer in the South, we see an increasing number of seersucker-themed gatherings. Guests attired in stripes, checks, and pastels arrive with packages for the host as they come to sip wine and enjoy the culinary tastes of the season. Seersucker, a thin, puckered cotton fabric, is light and cool and long associated with warm weather. So when it comes out of wardrobes and linen closets, you know summer's on its way. Seersucker is a traditional Southern fabric, making it a natural for this garden-inspired party.

I like to push aside the expected, in this case typical seersucker pastels. Instead, I selected a palette of hot coral with varying shades of blue, cream, and crisp white. Homeowners Kathryn and Paul Johnston had gorgeous blue-and-white porcelain throughout their traditional home, so I decided to make use of their treasures to build the place settings.

TIP

Try incorporating acrylic-handled flatware to add visual interest to place settings. Kim Seybert's acrylic, faceted flatware gave the table glamorous appeal.

One Enchanted Night

Florals are an important element of tablescape design. Not only do they kick up the elegance factor a notch, but they add life to the table. Coral garden roses, orange ranunculus, and blue hydrangeas were among the floral goodness supplied by Tanarah Luxe Floral.

Not enough room on your table and worried about blocking guests as they mingle? Try placing your larger arrangements on the buffet and keep tabletop florals low.

Cocktail Hour

I often set up a separate area for cock-tail hour. Giving guests a place to mingle, have drinks, and nibble on small plates lightens the mood and takes pressure off the host. Tiered serving trays work well to display and serve hors d'oeuvres while providing a ledge for candles or floral. Chef Janice Provost of Parigi fashioned a plethora of small bites for our guests.

TIP

Mixing florals and candles with hors d' oeuvres on multilevel serving trays adds to the ambience of a patio cocktail hour.

TIP

Locating cocktail hour on the patio shelters guests from the hustle and bustle of party prep in the dining room. I use this tactic often when entertaining.

Seersucker Social Recipes

Courtesy of Chef Janice Provost, Parigi

DEVILED QUAIL EGGS

Serves 6

18 quail eggs

2½ teaspoons mayonnaise

½ teaspoon Dijon mustard

Salt, to taste

2½ tablespoons crème fraiche

2 ounces caviar

2 teaspoons snipped fresh chives

Directions

Rinse the quail eggs in a colander. Place the eggs in a saucepan and cover with water. Bring to a boil and cook 4 minutes. Place eggs in an ice bath and peel. Cut one-sixteenth of an inch off bottom of eggs to create a stable base so they will stay upright. Cut top of egg, pop out the center, then mash yolk in a small bowl. Mix yolks with mayonnaise, mustard, and salt. Place mixture into a pastry bag and fill the whites with the yolk mixture. Cover with plastic until ready to serve. To serve, place a small amount of crème fraiche on top of yolk mixture. Top with caviar and chives.

TOMATO ASPIC WITH CRAB SALAD AND FRESH HERBS

Serves 6

Tomato Aspic

4 cups tomato juice

2 tablespoons lemon juice

½ onion, chopped

1 teaspoon sugar

½ cup apple cider vinegar

2 tablespoons unflavored powdered gelatin

2 teaspoons salt

Zest of one lemon

Directions

Place tomato juice, lemon juice, onion, and sugar in a medium saucepan and heat to a simmer. Combine the cider vinegar and gelatin, and stir into the tomato liquid, dissolving the gelatin completely. Stir in the salt and lemon zest. Ladle into 6 shallow bowls in 4-ounce portions. Cover and place in refrigerator to set for a minimum of 8 hours or overnight.

Crab Salad

1 pound lump crab

¼ cup mayonnaise

1 teaspoon lemon juice

Zest of half a lemon

2 tablespoons snipped chives

2 tablespoons tarragon, chopped

1 cup assorted garden herbs such as dill, parsley, cilantro, bronze fennel

Edible flowers, microgreens, nasturtium (optional)

Radishes thinly sliced for garnish (optional)

Directions

Pick through the crab, discarding any shells. In a bowl, mix the mayonnaise, lemon juice, lemon zest, chives, and tarragon. Fold crab into mayonnaise mixture, gently coating but not shredding it. Remove aspics from fridge. Place a spoonful of crab salad in a semicircle on top of each aspic, leaving space for herbs and flowers. Arrange herbs and flowers attractively, tucking them inside the crab salad.

BERKSHIRE PORK CHOP WITH SHERRY PAN BUTTER, FARRO–PETIT POIS–MUSHROOM RISOTTO, AND SAUTÉED SWISS CHARD

Serves 4

4 8-ounce Berkshire pork chops

Brine

½ cup kosher salt

1½ cups brown sugar

4 cloves garlic, crushed

1½ gallons cool water

Directions

Combine all ingredients except the pork chops to create the brine. Stir until the sugar and salt are dissolved. Place pork chops in brine and refrigerate 2–4 hours.

Sherry Pan Butter

Olive oil for frying

½ cup sherry

1½ cups chicken stock

2 tablespoons butter

Directions

Preheat the oven to 450 degrees. Remove the chops from the brine and pat dry. Heat a skillet over medium-high heat and coat pan with a little olive oil. Sear the chops on

both sides. Put chops in the oven and cook for 6–8 minutes. Remove the chops from the oven and allow to rest.

Deglaze the pan with the sherry and reduce to 1 tablespoon. Add the chicken stock and reduce by half. Swirl in the butter. Reserve for topping the chop.

Farro Risotto, part 1
Serves 4

1½ cups whole farro

3 cups chicken stock

3 cups water

2 tablespoons unsalted butter

½ onion, diced

1 clove garlic

Directions

Place farro in a food processor or blender and pulse about six times to break some of the farro into smaller pieces. In a stock pot, combine the stock and water; bring to a boil. Reduce heat to medium-low, keeping the liquid at a simmer. In a large, heavy-bottom pot, melt butter over medium heat. Sauté onion until softened. Add garlic and stir about 30 seconds. Add farro to onion and garlic, and stir to coat the grain; lightly toast 3-4 minutes. Pour 5 cups of the hot broth onto the farro and stir. Lower the heat and cook until the farro is al dente, stirring occasionally. Spread farro on a sheet pan to cool. You'll finish assembling the dish while the pork chop is cooking.

Farro Risotto, part 2

2 tablespoons olive oil

2 cup mushrooms, sliced

1 tablespoon chopped garlic

¼ cup sherry

½ cup petit pois, blanched

2 tablespoons butter

Salt and pepper

Set a medium sauté pan over medium-high heat and add oil, mushrooms, and garlic. Sauté about 2 minutes, taking care not to burn the garlic. Deglaze the pan with sherry and cook until liquid has evaporated. Add the cooked farro and the remaining cup of broth to the pan, stirring gently. Heat through. Add the petit pois and finish with the butter. Salt and pepper to taste. Serve farro under pork chop with swiss chard.

SAUTÉED SWISS CHARD

Serves 4

2 pounds swiss chard

¼ cup extra-virgin olive oil

1 cup shallots, thinly sliced

2 garlic cloves, minced

1 teaspoon hot chili flakes

¼ cup apple cider vinegar

¼ cup bacon, chopped and cooked crisp

3 tablespoons butter

Salt and pepper

Directions

Heat oil in a large sauté pan and add shallots and garlic. Cook until soft, about 5 minutes. Add chili flakes and cook for about a minute. Add swiss chard and sauté until tender, about 4 minutes. Add the vinegar and stir. Add the butter and swirl to melt. Toss with the crisp bacon, season with salt and pepper, and serve hot.

BREAD PUDDING

Serves 4

1 loaf cubed white bread

1 quart heavy cream

½ cup brown sugar

3 ounces chocolate chips

¼ cup pecans, chopped

Whipped cream for garnish

Edible flowers for garnish

Fresh berries for garnish

Mint for garnish

Set oven to 350 degrees. Cut the bread into bite-size cubes; place in a large mixing bowl. Add all the remaining ingredients to the bowl and mix with your hands until thoroughly combined. The consistency will be wet, almost like a lumpy pancake mix. Spray individual ramekins with nonstick spray and place the mixture in the dishes, pressing down tightly with a spatula. Cover with foil. Bake 45–60 minutes, watching carefully at the end. Cool on a wire rack. When ready to serve, top with whipped cream, fresh berries, mint, and edible flowers.

Poolside Soiree
in Hickory Hills

O ur dear friends the Erwins, O'Connors, and Cones had purchased a poolside dinner at our home at a Woman of Inspiration silent auction benefiting Children's Advocacy Centers of Arkansas. With the help of florist Angie Strange of Posh Floral in Dallas, Texas, I created an unforgettable chic poolside dinner for ten.

Chef Tim Morton of RH Catering created an elaborate dinner. Guests savored each divine course while eagerly anticipating the next dish.

Damask linens in moss green served as a blank canvas for our floral runner adorned with variegated pittosporum, lemon leaves, lemons, fuchsia ranunculus, Yellow Tree peonies, Coral Charm peonies, and white stock. Three statuesque arrangements featuring lemons and lemon leaves made a grand statement.

TIP

An opulent floral runner in lieu of low arrangements creates an impact. Consider placing clear glass hurricane candle holders on the runner for height.

• • •

Floral and Citrus

Lemons were integrated throughout the design in the runner, tall arrangements, and place cards.
I selected Royal Albert's Old Country Rose pattern for dinnerware. The china's floral motif
helped build the theme and, in this case, added color and pattern to the table.

Donna Cone

• • •

Divine Details

Lemons, sliced down the center and used as
place cards, added zest to the table setting.

TIP

*When using lemons as place
card holders, make sure to
select large, bright yellow
lemons. Small lemons tend
to be unstable and do not
work well as holders.*

menu

Amuse
FOIE GRAS TORCHON

First
CRAB MIMOSA SALAD

Second
SMOKED QUAIL WITH TOMATO & PEPPER JAM

Intermezzo
RASPBERRY LEMON SORBET

Main Course
CORIANDER CURED STEAK STRIP
SWEET POTATO PURÉE, COLLARD GREENS

Cheese Course
AGED CHEDDAR
COFFEE PECAN GLAZE

Dessert Course
LEMON BRÛLÉE QUENELLE
RASPBERRY, CHOCOLATE PLAQUE, CARAMELIZED GRAPEFRUIT,
ST. CECILIANI CREAM

Poolside Soiree Recipes

*Courtesey of Chef
Tim Morton, RH Catering*

CRAB MIMOSA SALAD

Serves 4

½ pound jumbo lump crab

1 red bell pepper, chopped

1 bunch green onions, chopped

Basil leaves, chopped

Bibb lettuce

Orange sections for garnish

Directions

Mix crab, bell pepper, green onions, and basil.
Serve salad in martini glasses lined with Bibb
lettuce. Garnish with orange sections.

Vinaigrette

1 egg yolk

¼ shallot

Fresh-squeezed lemon juice

1 cup rice wine vinegar

⅛ cup honey

2 cups extra-virgin olive oil

Salt and pepper

Directions

Place all ingredients except olive oil into
a blender and process for 30 seconds.
Add olive oil in a slow drizzle until the
dressing appears thick and milky. Add salt
and pepper to taste. Drizzle the dressing
over the Crab Mimosa Salad and serve
immediately.

SMOKED QUAIL
WITH TOMATO AND
PEPPER JAM

Serves 4

4 to 5 whole quail

Salt and pepper

Directions

Season quail liberally with salt and pepper.
Smoke in a smoker for 45 minutes.

Tomato and Pepper Jam

4 tomatoes, diced and drained

2 tablespoons bacon grease

½ Vidalia onion, chopped

4 jalapeño peppers

2 serrano peppers

2½ cups brown sugar

2 cloves

Grated Manchego cheese and fresh herbs
for quail garnish

Artisan lettuce for garnish

Directions

In a pot, add grease, onion, and peppers;
cook for 10 minutes. Add brown sugar and
cloves; reduce to a syrup. Add tomato and
simmer 10 minutes. Add water if needed.

To plate: Place pepper jam in center of plate
and swirl lightly around edge. Top with
grated Manchego and fresh herbs. Place a
quail in the center on top of the pepper jam.
Place lettuce between legs of bird.

CORIANDER-CURED
STEAK SERVED WITH
SWEET POTATO PURÉE
AND COLLARD GREENS

Serves 4

2–3 pounds skirt steak

Coriander cure

Coriander Cure

1 cup brown sugar

¼ cup fresh coriander seed

¼ cup kosher salt

1 tablespoon chili powder

½ tablespoon cumin

3 tablespoons olive oil

Mix all ingredients, adding olive oil last. Set aside.

Steak

Coat steaks with coriander cure, pressing to adhere. Heat pan to medium-high and place a tablespoon of oil in the pan. Season steaks with salt and pepper. Cook 7 minutes each side. Let rest for 12 minutes before slicing. Serve with sweet potato purée, steak sauce, and collard greens.

Sweet Potato Purée

4 sweet potatoes, peeled and baked

1 Idaho potato, peeled and baked

¼ cup heavy cream

½ cup maple syrup

1 teaspoon nutmeg

½ tablespoon roasted garlic

Salt to taste

Directions

Bake potatoes, cool, and peel. Place all ingredients into blender; blend until smooth and pass through a strainer.

Collard Greens

3 bunches collard greens, washed and chopped

1 whole onion, julienned

3 cloves garlic, thinly sliced

¼ pound fatback or bacon, diced

¼ cup sugar

¼ cup balsamic vinegar

1 jalapeño, whole

Directions

Sauté onion, garlic, and fatback; sweat for 5 to 10 minutes. Add sugar and balsamic vinegar; simmer for 1 minute. Add collard greens and jalapeño. Cover with water. Cook on medium heat for 45 minutes or until greens are tender.

Steak Sauce

1 cup Worcestershire

1 cup demi-glace

1 tablespoon horseradish

2 tablespoons butter

In a saucepan, reduce Worcestershire, demi-glace, and horseradish by half. Stir in butter. Strain and serve.

LEMON BRÛLÉE QUENELLE

Serves 6

12 egg yolks

3 cups sugar

1 quart heavy cream

1 tablespoon vanilla

Zest of 4 lemons

4 tablespoons sanding sugar

Lemon zest for garnish

Fresh raspberries for garnish

Whisk together all ingredients in a large bowl. Transfer into ramekins. Bake in a water bath at 375 degrees for 45 minutes. Cool on wire rack. Chill 4 hours or until ready to serve. Sprinkle with sanding sugar and torch with a kitchen torch until top is evenly melted and caramelized. Garnish with lemon zest and fresh raspberries.

Fourth of July
Poolside
Celebration

I f you've ever planned a Fourth of July celebration, you'll know what I mean when I say, there's a fine line to walk to keep it classy. The trick to an upscale Fourth of July is to steer clear of the conventional Stars and Stripes theme while working within the traditional Independence Day palette.

Find design elements in red, white, and blue that would not normally be included in Fourth of July entertaining, and you've mastered it. I'm certainly not saying you can't integrate a few of the traditional elements, but they needn't be the focal point. I tend to look at linen textiles first when building an event design; for this party, I worked from Thibaut's bold, cheerful patterns.

A color-blocked floating floral design is the perfect way to make a splash in the pool. Teresa and Dr. Joseph Murphy's rectangular pool called for a large floral arrangement in the center. Remember to anchor it so it doesn't drift.

TIP

Renting larger-scale furniture for a backyard bash provides extra seating and softens the look of the space. You should be able to get everything you need from your local event rental company. We selected Hanks Event Rentals because of its large inventory.

Explosion of COLOR!

Is there anything more amazing than the combination of red, white, and blue? Bold linens are trending, and the Fourth of July is an ideal occasion for making a statement with pattern. I selected Thibaut's Tanzania and Batik fabrics because of their striking patterns.

Kim Seybert's Flare napkin ring in cobalt and silver reminded me of shooting fireworks, and they coordinated delightfully with the raised pattern on our Alegria dinnerware from Skyros. Texture helps anchor a design, and Kim Seybert's beaded Navy Confetti placemats worked well as a foundation for the place settings.

TIP

I am a true believer in luxury stemware. It can make a dramatic difference when showcasing a wine's aroma. I selected glasses from Riedel's Veritas Collection.

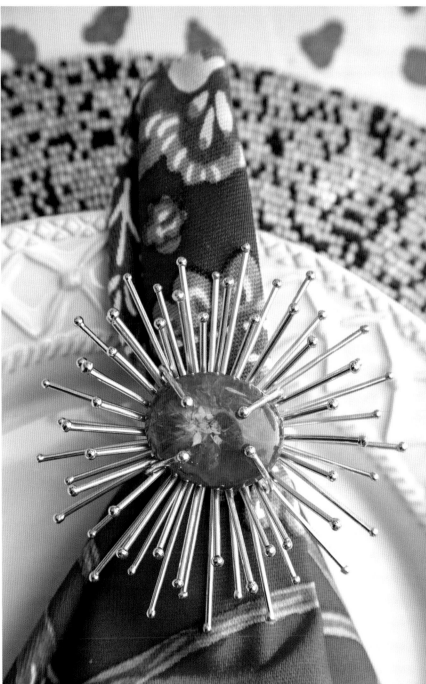

Pop, Bang, BOOM!

Colorblocking makes a tablescape statement and helps florals pop. A similar variety or color of floral stems grouped en masse creates an elegant yet contemporary display. The Silks A Bloom team in Little Rock, Arkansas, integrated tropical greenery, blue thistle, blue delphinium, red anemones, white hydrangeas, snapdragons, and Freedom Red roses.

FIRST

Red, White & Blue Salad

watermelon + goat feta + blueberries

toasted almonds + basil

SECOND

BBQ Pork Jowl Sliders

cheddar + gochujang mayo + crispy onions

THIRD

Chicken & Donuts

southern fried chicken + donuts + habanero-maple syrup

BANG!

Smoked Banana Pudding

homemade nillas + hickory smoked sea salt

Rock Town Bourbon chantilly

Fourth of July Recipes

Courtesy of Chef Scott Rains, Table 28

RED, WHITE, AND BLUE SALAD

Serves 6

1 baby watermelon

1 pound goat feta, ½-inch cubes

¾ cup extra-virgin olive oil

⅛ cup champagne vinegar

3 tablespoons honey

Juice of one lemon

Salt and pepper to taste

1 cup toasted marcona almonds

1 pint blueberries

1 tablespoon basil (preferably micro)

Directions

Cut watermelon and feta into ½-inch cubes. Mix olive oil and the champagne vinegar, honey, and lemon juice; season with salt and pepper. Toss the cubes of melon and cheese in the bowl to coat. Arrange on plates in a uniform square; garnish with toasted almonds, blueberries, and basil.

BBQ PORK JOWL

Serves 6

Pork jowl, shoulder, or belly

Olive oil

2 tablespoons paprika (smoked is best)

1 tablespoon garlic powder

1 teaspoon onion powder

1 teaspoon black pepper

1 teaspoon ground oregano

1 teaspoon cumin powder

1 teaspoon chili powder

1 teaspoon brown sugar

1 teaspoon salt

Directions

Heat a grill or prepare smoker. (If using a grill, consider adding hickory chips for flavor.) Mix dry ingredients together. Rub the jowls with olive oil and coat with dry rub mix. Smoke or grill 1–2 hours or until tender; check tenderness with fork. Wrap jowl in aluminum foil pouch; cook at 325 degrees for another hour. Assemble on slider buns with gochujang mayo, cheese, and crispy fried onions.

Optional: Coat jowls with BBQ sauce.

GOCHUJANG MAYO

1 cup Duke's mayonnaise

1 tablespoon gochujang chili paste

1 teaspoon smoked paprika

1 teaspoon cumin powder

1 teaspoon chili powder

Mix all ingredients until thoroughly combined.

SOUTHERN FRIED CHICKEN WITH DOUGHNUTS AND HABAÑERO MAPLE SYRUP

Serves 6

Fried Chicken

12 boneless chicken thighs or breasts

2 cups buttermilk

1 cup Frank's RedHot hot sauce (optional)

3 cups flour

1 tablespoon paprika

4 tablespoons poultry seasoning

1 tablespoon black pepper

1 tablespoon onion powder

1 tablespoon garlic powder

2 tablespoons salt

¼ teaspoon cayenne

4 cups shortening for frying

Mix buttermilk and hot sauce; pour over chicken and soak overnight. When you're ready to cook, mix flour with all the dry seasonings. Heat oil to 350 degrees. Dredge the chicken in seasoned flour. Fry until golden brown, 8–10 minutes depending on the thickness of chicken. Check with a thermometer to make sure the chicken has reached an internal temperature of 160 degrees. Let rest until it reaches 165 degrees, about 10 minutes.

Habañero Maple Syrup

1 cup maple syrup (warm)

1–2 habañero peppers, thinly sliced (seedless)

Add sliced habañeros to maple syrup and keep warm.

Doughnuts

¼ cup sugar

1⅛ cups whole milk (warm)

3 teaspoons instant yeast

2 large eggs

3 tablespoons melted butter

½ teaspoon vanilla

3¾ cups flour

1 teaspoon salt

4 cups vegetable shortening for frying

Glaze for Doughnuts

3 cups powdered sugar

½ teaspoon vanilla

½ teaspoon salt

¼ cup ice water

Directions

For doughnuts: Warm milk in saucepan. In a bowl, mix sugar and the warm milk, then add the yeast. Allow to sit for 15 minutes. In another bowl, beat the eggs and add the melted butter. Place butter and egg mixture in a standing electric mixer. Pour in the milk mixture and add vanilla. Mix at low speed with a hook attachment. Mix flour and salt in a bowl. Add the flour to the mixing bowl ½ cup at a time. Mix for 5 minutes. After flour is combined, put the dough in a lightly oiled bowl. Cover with wrap and refrigerate 8–12 hours.

Allow dough to come to room temperature for about 2 hours. Turn the dough onto a floured surface. Cut out doughnuts with a cookie or doughnut cutter. Separate

the hole from the doughnut. Let them rise again for about 2 hours. Melt the shortening in a pot or deep fryer and heat to 350 degrees. Add the dough to the oil, pushing it down into the oil with a spatula and turning it over until golden brown on both sides, 1–2 minutes per side. Cool on a wire rack.

For glaze: Mix the powdered sugar with the vanilla; add salt to taste. Add ice water and mix until smooth. Pour glaze over doughnuts; place a tray underneath to catch extra glaze.

SMOKED BANANA PUDDING WITH HOMEMADE VANILLA WAFERS AND BOURBON WHIPPED CREAM

Serves 6

Vanilla Pudding

4 tablespoons flour

1½ cups sugar

1 teaspoon smoked sea salt

3 large eggs

3 cups milk

1 teaspoons vanilla

Directions

Combine flour, sugar, and smoked sea salt in a heavy saucepan. Beat eggs and combine with the milk. Add to dry ingredients in the saucepan and cook over low heat, stirring constantly until ingredients thicken, 8–10 minutes. Add vanilla and remove from heat. Chill

Homemade Vanilla Wafers

1 cup unsalted butter

2 cups sugar

2 eggs

4 teaspoons vanilla extract

2 teaspoons baking powder

2½ cups all-purpose flour

2 tablespoons milk

Pinch of salt

Directions

Preheat oven to 350 degrees. Beat together butter and sugar. Add eggs, vanilla, and baking powder. Beat until smooth and fluffy. Add flour, milk, and salt and mix until combined. Use two spoons to drop teaspoon-size dollops of batter onto a greased baking sheet. Bake until light brown, 6–7 minutes. Allow to cool.

Bourbon Whipped Cream

2 cups heavy cream

½ cup powdered sugar

2 teaspoons vanilla

Pinch smoked sea salt

2 tablespoons bourbon

Directions

Mix cream with a whisk or electric mixer. Once cream starts to thicken, add powdered sugar, vanilla, salt, and bourbon. Beat until light and fluffy. Chill before serving.

Garnish

6 tablespoons butter

1 cup brown sugar

6 bananas, sliced

Smoked sea salt

Directions

Melt butter and brown sugar together on low. Add sliced bananas and cook until slightly brown.

Assembly: Place vanilla wafers on a plate; top with vanilla pudding, bourbon whipped cream, and banana garnish. Add chocolate shavings and a pinch of smoked sea salt.

Under the Sea
Dinner on the Reef

S eafood just happens to be my favorite food, so I was inspired to design an Under the Sea theme featuring Chef Payne Harding's creations from Cache Restaurant in Little Rock.

My home is traditional in design so I wanted to keep florals traditional, but I also wanted to evoke images of the sea with a reef-inspired theme. Tanarah Haynie of Tanarah Lux Floral collaborated with me to design florals in my John Richard silver-and-gold seashell footed containers. By the end of the day, my French dining room was transformed for an enchanted evening under the sea.

TIP

A mix of seashells and shell-shaped containers brings the undersea theme to life.

Table Talk

Intricately beaded Kim Seybert place-mats in gold and cream set the tone for a sophisticated evening. I used oyster-shells with gold gilded edges as place cards and had guests' names written in calligraphy. The shells were decorative and functional and served as a special takeaway for guests. Napkin rings adorned with resin reef detailing set on acrylic were also sea-party worthy.

TIP

Oystershells work well as place cards. Try painting the edges gold and the interior a pearlized sheer cream. Write the guests' names in metallic gold calligraphy.

Enchanting Details

From napkins to stemware, details are everything when entertaining. Kim Seybert's embroidered reef napkins coordinate with our other sea-inspired décor.

Gold, silver, and champagne metals catch the light on a tablescape. The place settings' touches of gold complement the gold gilded detail of my Henredon dining room chairs.

TIP

I often mix metals to add glimmer. There are touches of gold on my stemware, place cards, napkins, and placemats. On the opposite end of the spectrum, silver also meandered through our centerpiece containers.

Ocean Vibes

An ambience fit for sea life comes together with silver-painted monstera leaves, Spanish moss, ocean song roses, hot-pink tulips, purple hydrangeas, blue thistle, calla lilies, and other floral varieties. Guests are treated to edible menus designed by Carmen Potillo of Coco Belle Chocolates.

TIP

Edible menus satisfy the sweet tooth. Hire a professional chocolatier to make this memorable delight.

TIP

Chocolate menus tend to melt quickly. Have clear plastic bags and ribbon ready for guests to tuck them away after reading.

Under the Sea Recipes

Courtesy of Chef Payne Harding, Cache Restaurant

SEARED CHILEAN SEA BASS WITH SAFFRON CREAM SAUCE

Per serving

1 fillet of sea bass
Salt and pepper
1 tablespoon butter
Bunch of spinach
4 tablespoons olive oil, divided
Small fingerling potatoes
3 sprigs of thyme

Cream Sauce
Serves 6

8 ounces coconut milk
1 tablespoon butter
2 pinches fresh saffron
1 bay leaf
8 ounces heavy cream
Salt and pepper to taste
Kaluga caviar for garnish

Directions

Season sea bass with salt and pepper to taste. Place the sea bass skin-side down in a hot pan with butter. Turn it and cook it a few minutes longer. Transfer sea bass to a plate to rest. Meanwhile, sauté spinach in olive oil and keep warm. Preheat oven to 450 degrees. Cut potatoes tourne style and cook in boiling water. Drain. Heat olive oil in a pan and add thyme over medium or medium-low to infuse the flavor. Put potatoes back in pan and coat with the thyme oil, and salt and pepper to taste. Put in a baking dish and bake until the sides are golden brown.

Saffron cream sauce: Place coconut milk and butter in a pan and crumble in saffron. Add bay leaf and let it steep until the saffron colors the milk. Add the cream, bring to a boil, and reduce until the sauce coats the back of a spoon. Salt and pepper to taste. Plate sea bass on top of the spinach and place potatoes on the side with caviar as a garnish. Drizzle sauce on fish and serve hot.

CRAB TOWER

Serves 4

Crab

1 pound lump crab

2 tablespoons chopped chives

2 tablespoons olive oil

Salt to taste

Tumeric oil for garnish

Basil oil for garnish

Toss lump crab with chives, olive oil, and salt; set aside and chill.

Guacamole

9 medium avocados

3 tablespoons red onion

3 tablespoons jalapeño

3 tablespoons lime

3 tablespoons cilantro

Salt and pepper to taste

Mix everything in a blender until smooth. Chill.

Compressed Mango

Put 3 cups diced mango and 1 tablespoon simple syrup in vacuum bag and seal with vacuum machine at full pressure. If you do not have a vacuum machine, place mangos and simple syrup in a zippered bag and chill in refrigerator for 1 hour.

In a 3–4-inch round tin mold, layer the guacamole, crab mixture, and compressed mango. Top with microgreens. Drizzle turmeric oil and basil oil over the crab tower and serve.

VANILLA BEAN PANNA COTTA WITH RASPBERRY COULIS AND MANGO SORBET

Orange gelee

9 gelatin sheets

Ice water

4 cups orange juice

½ cup sugar

Bloom 9 gelatin sheets in ice water. Mix gelatin, orange juice, and sugar in a heavy pan; bring to a simmer. Set in sheet tray and chill for 4 hours. Slice into 4-inch squares once set and leave in tray until serving.

Mango sorbet

16 ounces mangos

3 ounces simple syrup

2 ounces lime juice

Purée mango, water, simple syrup, and lime juice. Place mixture in the freezer and freeze.

Raspberry coulis

2 pints raspberries

1 cup sugar

1 tablespoon cornstarch

5 ounces water

Heat raspberries, sugar, cornstarch, and water in a small saucepan over medium heat, stirring occasionally, until the sugar dissolves. Place mixture in a blender or food processor and purée. Strain through a fine-mesh sieve to remove the seeds. Chill.

Granola

3 cups oats

1 cup brown sugar

¾ cup dried cranberries

½ cup butter, melted

1 teaspoon vanilla

¼ cup pure maple syrup

Combine oats, brown sugar, dried cranberries, butter, and vanilla. Toss with maple syrup. Roast mixture on a buttered sheet tray at 325 degrees 15–20 minutes.

Panna cotta

3 gelatin sheets

Ice water

2 cups buttermilk

1 cup heavy cream

1 cup sugar

½ teaspoon lemon zest

1 vanilla bean

Bloom 3 gelatin sheets in ice water. In saucepan, mix gelatin with buttermilk, heavy cream, sugar, lemon zest, and vanilla bean; bring to a simmer. Remove vanilla bean and strain to remove seeds. Pour panna cotta into preferred dish and chill 4 hours.

To serve, place orange gelee over set panna cotta. Place a scoop of mango sorbet on gelee. Spoon raspberry coulis over mango sorbet. Top with granola and garnish with fresh raspberries.

Fall

Fall Fest
at an English Estate

S tepping into Goodwin Manor feels like entering a traditional English estate, though it is in Little Rock, Arkansas. At the foothills of the Ouachita Mountains, the expansive country estate is a hidden treasure that offers year-round views of lush forests and hills. Owned by Andrea and Gary Goodwin, the home is roughly 15,000 square feet. More than 1,800 tons of field stone quarried at Hackett, Arkansas, were used to build the exterior and interior of this impressive home.

When I think of a Fall Fest dinner, I picture fruit, fall leaves, wheat, and a variety of florals. Rich in color, our design for this event included blue-and-white Wedgwood Renaissance fine china and floral arrangements overflowing with grapes, pears, pomegranates, wheat, foraged greenery, boxwood, peach roses, and blue hydrangeas. Multicolored napkins and a runner made from Thibaut's Navesink and Tazina patterns created a lasting impression of elegance.

TIP

Mixing varieties of fruit adds color, spatial interest, and dimension to a tablescape. Try pomegranates, grapes, pears, and apples for opulent yet down-to-earth centerpieces.

Dinner by Candlelight

A floral display with a myriad of colors seemed fitting for this fête. I called on Tanarah Haynie of Tanarah Luxe Floral to build the centerpieces. We decided on low arrangements in the center of the table flanked with taller, stately arrangements in aged pedestals to add height. Blue taper candles create a meandering path of color through the tablescape.

Chef Jaime McAfee of Pine Bluff Country Club presented an amazing menu of fall favorites.

TIP

Florals and greenery atop pedestals add height and drama to tablescapes.

FUN FACT

Pine Bluff Country Club is a hidden Arkansas gem. Chef Jaime is an award-winning talent who could practice anywhere in the world, yet selects Pine Bluff Country Club as his home.

◆ ◆ ◆

A mixture of rustic and classic elements added character to the tablescape
and acknowledged the home's architecture. Our aged pedestals and pots
complemented the room's rough-hewn stone fireplace.

"Autumn, the year's last,
loveliest smile."
          —William Cullen Bryant

• • •

Finishing Touches

Pomegranates adorned with gold calligraphy served as place cards and treasured takeaways for guests.
Gold flatware gave the table a warm glow and coordinated with the gold rims of the Wedgwood
Renaissance china.

Menu

SOUP
BUTTERNUT SQUASH ACCENTED WITH GINGER

SALAD
BRUSSEL SPROUTS PAIRED WITH THE BRIGHT FALL FLAVORS OF PEPPERED BACON,
PECANS, SHALLOTS, APPLES, AND POMEGRANATES,
TOPPED WITH GOAT CHEESE AND A MAPLE BALSAMIC VINAIGRETTE

ENTRÉE
ROASTED BEEF TENDERLOIN SERVED WITH A ROSEMARY INFUSED ROOT STACK
and
LAMB LOLLIPOP PAIRED WITH CRANBERRY BASMATI RICE AND CURRY SAUCE

DESSERT
PUMPKIN CHEESECAKE WITH A WARM RASPBERRY GLAZE

Fall Fest Recipes

*Courtesy of
Chef Jamie McAfee,
Pine Bluff Country Club*

FALL BRUSSELS SPROUTS SALAD

Serves 6

12 ounces brussels sprouts, outer leaves removed

¼ cup dried cranberries and fresh pomegranate seeds

¼ cup pecans

¼ cup gorgonzola cheese crumbles

1 pear, chopped

3 tablespoons extra-virgin olive oil

2 jumbo shallots, thinly sliced

Directions

Using a very sharp knife, thinly shred Brussels sprouts while holding on to the core end, then discard cores and add shredded sprouts to a large bowl with dried cranberries and pomegranate seeds, pecans, gorgonzola cheese, and chopped pear. Set aside. Heat olive oil in a skillet over medium-high heat. Add half the shallots and fry until light golden brown. Scoop onto a paper towel–lined plate to drain, then repeat with remaining shallots. Sprinkle with salt, then cool slightly.

Maple-Balsamic Vinaigrette

2 tablespoons extra-virgin olive oil

2 tablespoons balsamic vinegar

1 tablespoon real maple syrup

1 teaspoon Dijon mustard

Salt and pepper

Place ingredients in a jar and shake to combine.

To serve, pour vinaigrette over salad. Add fried shallots, toss to combine. Serve.

LAMB LOLLIPOPS WITH CRANBERRY BASMATI RICE AND CURRY SAUCE

Serves 6

1 pound lamb chops, frenched (or substitute 1 pound pork chops)

1 cup brown sugar

½ tablespoon ground ginger

3 cloves garlic, minced

¼ cup soy sauce

¼ cup Worchestershire sauce

1 tablespoon all-purpose house seasoning*

2 tablespoons olive oil

Parsley, chopped for garnish

Green onion, chopped for garnish

*House seasoning: Mix equal parts granulated garlic, Tony's seasoning, black pepper, and parsley flakes.

Directions

Whisk together brown sugar, ginger, garlic, soy sauce, Worcestershire sauce, and house seasoning. Place lamb chops in a plastic bag and pour marinade over chops. Seal and massage ingredients. Marinate in the refrigerator 4–6 hours. Using a large nonstick or cast-iron skillet, heat oil over medium-high heat. Remove lamb chops from marinade and shake off excess. Sear chops in pan, about 2 minutes each side. Allow to rest. Bring marinade to a rolling boil in a saucepan and reduce until thickened. Brush on chops after cooking. Remove and garnish with chopped parsley and green onion. Serve immediately.

Cranberry Basmati Rice
Serves 6

1 medium butternut squash, peeled, seeded,
and diced

2 tablespoons olive oil

Salt and pepper

3 tablespoons butter

2 cloves garlic, minced

1 large onion, diced

1¼ cups basmati rice

2 cups chicken or vegetable broth

½ cup dried cranberries

1 tablespoon minced fresh sage

1 teaspoon minced fresh thyme

Directions

Preheat oven to 425 degrees. Toss the butternut squash with the olive oil, salt, and pepper, then spread into one layer on a baking sheet. Bake 10–15 minutes, or until fork tender. Set aside. In a saucepan melt the butter over medium-high heat. Add garlic and onion and cook until just fragrant and tender, about 5 minutes. Add the rice, stirring to coat all grains. Add broth and bring to a boil. Reduce heat to low, cover, and cook undisturbed 15–20 minutes, or until the liquid is absorbed. Remove from heat and let rest for 5 minutes. Fluff with fork. Add the butternut squash, dried cranberries, sage, thyme, and salt and pepper to taste. Stir to combine.

Curry Sauce
Serves 6

1 tablespoon red curry paste

1 tablespoon fish sauce (optional)

1 15-ounce can coconut milk

2–3 tablespoons olive oil

1 teaspoon grated ginger

1 teaspoon grated garlic

1 onion, finely chopped

A few broccoli florets

1–2 carrots

½ red bell pepper

½ yellow bell pepper

1 teaspoon crushed black pepper

1 teaspoon red chili powder

1 teaspoon curry powder

1 bunch cilantro, chopped

Salt and pepper

Directions

In a bowl, combine red curry paste, fish sauce, and coconut milk. Stir well to make sure there are no lumps, and set aside. Heat a pan on medium-high heat. Add a tablespoon of oil and sauté grated ginger and garlic for a minute. Add onion and sauté until translucent. Add broccoli and sauté for a minute. Add carrots and thinly sliced red and yellow bell pepper. Mix well and cook the vegetables, covered, 2–3 minutes. Add the prepared sauce to the vegetables. Stir in black pepper and red chili powder and bring to a boil. Reduce heat and let simmer 5 minutes. Add curry powder and mix well. Sprinkle with cilantro, mix well, and remove from heat. Salt and pepper to taste.

BUTTERNUT SQUASH SOUP TOPPED WITH GINGER CREAM

Serves 6

4 pounds butternut squash, peeled, seeded, and cubed

1 large onion, roughly chopped

½-inch piece of fresh ginger, peeled, roughly sliced

¼ teaspoon nutmeg

4 cups vegetable stock

Olive oil

Salt and pepper to taste

Directions

In a large, deep pan, sauté onion over medium heat, softening with the salt and pepper. When the onions are soft, scoot them aside and tumble in some of the squash cubes and let brown for about 10 minutes, stirring occasionally. Add the rest of the squash, along with the ginger, nutmeg, and stock. Simmer until the squash is cooked. Pour mixture into food processor or a large blender and purée. Return to pot. Salt and pepper to taste. To serve, top with ginger cream.

Tip: Add maple syrup to sweeten if desired.

Ginger Cream

¼ cup Greek yogurt

3 tablespoons heavy whipping cream

1 teaspoon honey

½ teaspoon ground ginger

⅛ teaspoon salt

Directions

Pour yogurt and whipping cream into a bowl and whip with a hand mixer. Add honey, ginger, and salt and continue whipping until combined. Place a teaspoon of mixture on each serving of soup. Use a toothpick to create a fall design.

ROAST BEEF TENDERLOIN WITH ROSEMARY-INFUSED ROOT STACK

Serves 6

1 whole beef tenderloin, 4–5 pounds

4 tablespoons salted butter, or more to taste

2 tablespoons chopped garlic

2 tablespoons house seasoning*

Vegetable oil

***House seasoning:** Mix equal parts granulated garlic, Tony's seasoning, black pepper, and parsley flakes.

Directions

Preheat oven to 475 degrees. Rinse meat well. Trim away some of the fat to remove the silvery cartilage underneath. Sprinkle both sides generously with house seasoning and rub in with fingers. Heat vegetable oil in a heavy skillet. When the oil reaches the smoking point, place the tenderloin in the hot pan to sear it. Throw a couple of tablespoons of butter into the skillet. When one side is starting to brown, flip and repeat. Place the tenderloin in a roasting pan with a rack. Put several tablespoons of butter all over the meat. Stick a thermometer lengthwise into the meat. Roast until the temperature reaches just under 140 degrees, 15–20 minutes. Keep checking the meat thermometer to make sure it doesn't overcook. Let meat stand 10 minutes or so before slicing. To serve, spoon the olive oil / butter juices from the skillet onto the top of the meat.

Rosemary-Infused Root Stack

Choose whatever root vegetables you like. Slice them thin and toss with olive oil, rosemary, salt, and pepper. Place on a sheet pan and roast at 400 degrees for 15–20 minutes or until golden.

PUMPKIN CHEESECAKE WITH WARM RASPBERRY GLAZE

Serves 6

Crust

2 cups graham crackers food-processed to a fine texture

3 tablespoons light brown sugar

1 teaspoon cinnamon

1 stick salted butter, melted

Directions

In medium bowl, combine graham cracker crumbs, sugar, and cinnamon. Mix in melted butter. Firmly press mixture into a 9-inch springform pan. Set aside.

Cheesecake

3 8-ounce packages cream cheese, softened in microwave

1 15-ounce can pumpkin purée

1 cup granulated sugar

½ teaspoon cinnamon

⅛ teaspoon clove and nutmeg

1 teaspoon vanilla

1 can Eagle Brand condensed milk

½ cup whipping cream

4 eggs at room temperature

Directions

Preheat oven to 375 degrees. In a stand mixer, beat cream cheese until smooth and creamy. Add pumpkin purée, sugar, spices, vanilla, condensed milk, and whipping cream. Beat until well combined. Slowly add the eggs, keeping speed on low to avoid over-mixing. Pour mixture into prepared crust and spread out evenly. Bake in a water bath 45–60 minutes. Cheesecake is done when it is firm and the center jiggles. Turn oven off and let cool 30 minutes with the oven ajar. Remove from the oven and let cool on a wire rack. Cover with plastic wrap and place in refrigerator for at least 4 hours to set.

Raspberry Glaze

2 pounds fresh raspberries

½ cup sugar

⅔ cup water

2 teaspoons lemon juice

1 tablespoon cornstarch

Directions

Combine raspberries, sugar, water, and lemon juice in a large saucepan on high heat. Stir thoroughly while bringing to a boil. After the mixture begins to boil, reduce the heat to low and cook for up to 10 minutes, stirring occasionally. As the raspberries soften, use a wooden spoon to break them in pieces to release the flavor. Remove from heat. Using a strainer, pour liquid into a bowl, pressing the juices through the strainer with a wooden spoon. Dispose of solid raspberries left over from mixture and return liquid to pan on low heat. Meanwhile, whisk the cornstarch with 3 tablespoons water in a small bowl. Pour into the simmering pan of raspberry juice. Increase heat to high and continue to whisk until it thickens into a glaze, 3–5 minutes.

Elegant Cabin
Dinner at Split River

Even on a weekday, a drive to the Arkansas River cabin of Sharri and Bill Jones feels like a lazy Sunday in the country. A dirt road meanders past cattle, deer, and green pastures. A stop or two may be necessary as a cow decides to play greeter, and you'd better not be in a hurry because farmers will want to stop and talk about the weather.

Southern Arkansas has a welcoming culture that is exemplified in the owners' down-to-earth personalities. Bill, Sharri, and Bill's dear mother, Sissy, who also own Sissy's Log Cabin, a fine jewelry store chain, have become well-known in Arkansas through the years. When they decided to expand their storefronts, I was comissioned to design the new locations in Arkansas and Tennessee.

Scott and I have enjoyed many weekends at the Joneses' Arkansas River home, which they lovingly call Split River, and I wanted to make it a cozy venue for a fall event. Chef Jamie McAfee of Pine Bluff Country Club catered a delightful multicourse meal.

TIP

Lifting a tall arrangement off the table makes a grand statement without blocking conversation. The towering centerpiece by Tanarah Haynie of Tanarah Luxe Floral rests on a sheet of clear glass positioned on three tall glass vases.

"The quiet rhythmic monotone of the wall of logs fills one with the rustic peace of a secluded nook in the woods."
—Gustav Stickley

· · ·

Want to create an elegant yet cozy place setting fit for a cabin? Try a placemat such as Kim Seybert's Fossil design and work in a few deer shed (antlers) on the table. Place cards in wood-chip stands also provide casual appeal with a formal touch.

Layer it UP

I love to layer more than one pattern and manufacturer when dressing a table. For the base, I started with Kim Seybert's Fossil design placemat and layered with Skyros Isabella Ice Blue dinnerware. Sharri's Spode dishes in the Woodlands pattern topped off the place setting.

The pale-blue sky in the Woodlands pattern co-ordinates perfectly with our ice-blue dinnerware. Nestled between the plates, a Thibaut fabric napkin complements the placemat and echoes the green in the Spode bowl.

TIP •

Don't be afraid to mix and match dinnerware patterns. Layering opens up a new world of possibilities when dressing the table.

TIP

Look for unusual flatware. We used Spode Woodlands flatware in a coordinating pattern to Sharri's dinnerware. Embellished with game birds and British flowers, the Woodlands flatware worked perfectly with our theme.

Cozy Elegance

Pine cones, deer shed (antlers), and candlelight create ambience for an elegant evening at Split River Cabin. For drama, amaranthus draped from tall centerpieces lends a feeling of being in a lush forest or near a waterfall. The arrangements laden with coral roses, greens, and hypericum berries complemented the low pine cones and green hydrangeas in resin wood containers.

Soup

A CLASSIC COLD POTATO LEEK SOUP PAIRED
WITH A WARM TURNIP VICHYSSOISE

Salad

CAESAR SALAD TOPPED WITH
A SALT-CURED EGG YOLK

Entrée

ROASTED QUAIL STUFFED WITH WILD DUCK.
RICE AU GRATIN AND SERVED WITH TARRAGON
INFUSED HEIRLOOM CARROT BUNDLES

Dessert

CARAMEL PECAN TART TOPPED WITH
A FALL ACCENTED WHIP CREAM

Elegant Cabin Recipes

Courtesy of
Chef Jamie McAfee,
Pine Bluff Country Club

CARAMEL PECAN TART

Serves 6

3½ cups coarsely chopped pecans

2 cups all-purpose flour

⅔ cup powdered sugar

¾ cup butter, cubed

½ cup firmly packed brown sugar

½ cup honey

⅔ cup butter

3 tablespoons whipping cream

Directions

Preheat oven to 350 degrees. Arrange pecans in a single layer on a baking sheet. Bake 5–7 minutes or until lightly toasted. Cool on a wire rack.

Pulse flour, powdered sugar, and ¾ cup butter in a food processor 5 to 6 times or until mixture resembles coarse meal. Pat mixture evenly on bottom and up sides of a lightly greased 11-inch tart pan with removable bottom. Bake at 350 degrees for 20 minutes or until edges are lightly browned. Cool on a wire rack 15 minutes or until completely cool.

Bring the brown sugar, honey, ⅔ cup butter, and whipping cream to a boil in a 3-quart saucepan over medium-high heat. Stir in toasted pecans, and spoon hot filling into prepared crust. Bake 25–30 minutes or until golden and bubbly. Cool on a wire rack.

SWEET POTATO BISCUITS

Serves 6

¾ cup cooked mashed sweet potato

⅓–½ cup whole milk, as needed

1½ cups all-purpose flour, plus more for dusting (gluten-free optional)

2 tablespoons sugar

1 tablespoon baking powder

1 teaspoon salt

2 tablespoons cold unsalted butter, cut into small bits

Directions

Preheat oven to 425 degrees. Grease baking sheet with butter, oil, or cooking spray. In a small bowl, whisk together the sweet potato and milk. Set aside. In a large bowl, whisk together dry ingredients. Cut in the butter with a pastry cutter or fork until the mixture resembles coarse meal. Add the sweet potato mixture and gently fold to combine. Add the remaining milk a little at a time until all of the flour is moistened.

Sprinkle a small handful of flour on a work surface. Turn the dough out onto the surface and knead lightly 2–3 times with the palm of your hand until the dough comes together. Pat the dough out into a ½-inch-thick round. Use a 2½-inch round biscuit cutter to cut the dough into biscuits. Gently roll the scraps and cut out more biscuits. Place on prepared baking sheet and bake 12–20 minutes, depending on oven, until light golden brown and firm to the touch. Serve warm or at room temperature.

VICHYSSOISE CLASSIC

Serves 6

3 cups peeled, sliced potatoes

3 cups sliced white of leek, washed well

1½ quarts chicken broth

½–1 cup whipping cream

Salt and white pepper to taste

2–3 tablespoons minced chives

Directions

Simmer the vegetables in the broth until tender, 40–50 minutes. Purée the soup in a blender or put through a food mill and then a fine sieve. Stir in the cream and season to taste, oversalting slightly; salt loses savor in a cold dish. Chill. Garnish with chives.

CAESAR SALAD TOPPED WITH SALT-CURED EGG YOLK

Serves 4

2 large egg yolks

1 teaspoon Worcestershire sauce

2 teaspoons fresh-squeezed lemon juice

2 anchovy fillets, rinsed and patted dry

4 cloves garlic, peeled and minced

½ cup extra-virgin olive oil

½ teaspoon salt

2 heads romaine lettuce, torn into bite-size pieces

½ cup parmesan cheese, shredded

2 cups croutons

Directions

To make the dressing, whisk egg yolks, Worcestershire sauce, lemon juice, anchovies, and garlic. Slowly whisk in the oil. Season with salt and pepper to taste.

Salt-Cured Egg Yolks

1¾ cups kosher salt

1¼ cups sugar

4 large egg yolks

Nonstick vegetable oil spray

In a medium bowl, combine the salt and sugar. Spread half in a small baking dish. Make four evenly spaced indentations in the salt mixture. Carefully place a raw egg yolk in each depression. Sprinkle the remaining salt mix over top of the yolks, making sure they are completely covered. Cover tightly with plastic wrap and refrigerate for 4 days. Gently brush the salt off each egg and rinse under cool running water to remove the remaining salt. The yolk will have a gummy texture. Gently pat dry with a paper towel. Preheat oven to 150 degrees. Spray a wire rack with vegetable oil, place eggs on top, and set the rack on top of a baking sheet. Place in oven and turn oven off. Allow the yolks to dry out in the unheated oven for 2 days.

ROASTED QUAIL

Serves 4

4 quail breasts

Salt and pepper

Rosemary

Garlic powder

Butter

Spatchcock the quail by putting each quail breast-side down on a board; using scissors, cut through both sides of the backbone and lift it out. Using the flat of your hand, press firmly on the quail to flatten it. Rinse and pat dry. Season the quail with salt, pepper, rosemary, and garlic powder. Heat a medium sauté pan over high heat. Add butter to the pan, followed by the quail, breast down. Cook quail without moving them for about 5 minutes, then carefully flip and baste well with melted butter. Cook on the second side for 5 minutes, or until the quail is firm and tender. Let rest 5 minutes before serving.

Buerre Blanc

½ cup white wine

1 small shallot, chopped

1½ sticks chilled, unsalted butter

Salt and pepper to taste

Fresh herbs to taste

Lemon juice to taste

Simmer wine with the shallot in a medium skillet until there's just a little liquid left (about 2 tablespoons). Over low heat, whisk in the butter, a few pieces at a time, until the sauce is glossy and emulsified. Season with salt and pepper, a handful of chopped fresh herbs, and fresh lemon juice.

DUCK AU GRATIN RICE

Serves 4

4 cups cold cooked wild rice

½ cup celery

¼ cup green onions

¼ cup toasted shaved almonds

¼ cup grated parmesan cheese

2 cups heavy cream

Cooked ground duck (optional)

Directions

Preheat oven to 375 degrees. Sauté celery, onions, and almonds 3–5 minutes. Add parmesan and cream, place in a casserole dish, and bake until set. Optional: Add ground duck and bake 20–30 minutes.

TARRAGON-INFUSED CARROT BUNDLES

Serves 4

2 pounds whole baby carrots

2 tablespoons olive oil or butter

¼ cup honey

½ teaspoon black pepper

½ teaspoon kosher salt

2 tablespoons fresh tarragon

Directions

Blanch whole carrots until fork tender. Place carrots in an ice bath to cool. Sauté carrots in butter, honey, black pepper, and salt until carrots are warm enough to eat. Add tarragon and serve.

Oktoberfest
Backyard
Biergarten Bash

Oktoberfest dates back to 1810, when Crown Prince Ludwig of Bavaria married Princess Therese of Saxe-Hildburghausen. The original festival to honor the newlyweds included horse races, a variety of spectacles, royal pageantry, and, of course, wine and beer tastings. Today, the festival in Munich boasts more than six million attendees during a two-week period and has expanded to include carnival rides, musical entertainment, and more.

If you aren't able to hop on a plane and grab a beer in Munich, you can join in the fun by hosting your own backyard Oktoberfest bash.

Shay and Brian Geyer of Dallas, Texas, have a passion for cooking. Shay, an interior designer by day, has become an accomplished chef in her own kitchen by night as she whips up creative and beautiful dishes. I was thrilled to have the opportunity to design an Oktoberfest-inspired event in her stunning backyard and to experience her culinary skills firsthand.

TIP

Incorporate stemware with colored stems to coordinate with your theme. I selected the Intermezzo Blue pattern from Orrefors because of the blue drop in the glass stem. This detail was striking against Shay's backlit onyx table.

◆ ◆ ◆

Fall in Love

A mix of fall colors highlight the center of the table, while lapis-and-white Skyros dinnerware in the Villa Beleza pattern is layered around the perimeter. I knew we should integrate the official colors of Oktoberfest, which are blue and white, but I also wanted to mix in orange, green, and gold to lend an air of warmth. Tanarah Luxe Floral provided our dining area florals, which included orange roses, sunflowers, maple leaves, and fern. Our napkins in Thibaut's Blue Waterford pattern married well with our fall floral. A brushed gold napkin ring from Kim Seybert provided the finishing touch as the jewelry for our table.

• • •

Cheers

Shay's beer flights were genius and offered guests the opportunity to try a variety of brews
throughout the night. Sunflowers arranged in blue-and-white porcelain from Botanical Mix in
Dallas made an inviting backdrop to the beer-tasting station.

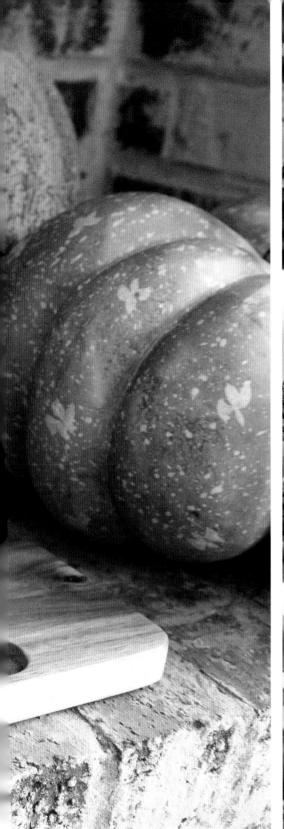

"In the entire circle of the year there are no days so delightful as those of a fine October."
—*Alexander Smith*

A Hearty Spread

The key to a successful biergarten bash is to provide a variety of culinary favorites. Guests were treated to a spread fit for a king that included Bavarian Beer Roasted Pork, Pretzel Bites with Beer Cheese Sauce, and Sauerkraut.

TIP

Beer doesn't have to be the only German beverage of the night. Glühwein (hot German spiced wine) is abundant with fall flavors. Try serving it in copper mugs garnished with cinnamon sticks and orange slices.

Be My Guest

A buffet with multilevel serving trays displayed an array of meats, cheeses, breads, fruits, and spreads. Multilevel trays help draw the eye upward and offer a dramatic and practical presentation option for food. We garnished Shay's with sunflower stems. Did you know that sunflowers are edible? From seed to stalk, they work perfectly as a garnish for fall dishes.

TIP

High and low candles running down the center of the table for a nighttime dinner party encourage conversation and add ambience. We selected a mixture of copper, gold, silver, and brown mercury glass containers for dimension and depth.

Cocktails

[...]
[...]
[...]

Appetizers

FALL CHARCUTERIE

PRETZEL BITES WITH
BEER CHEESE SAUCE

SAUSAGE AND
SAUERKRAUT
PHYLLO TURNOVERS

First Course

HOT GERMAN
POTATO SALAD

GERMAN WALDORF
SALAD

Main Course

ASSORTED SAUSAGES
AND BRATS FROM
BAVARIAN MEATS
IN SEATTLE, WA

CARMELIZED ONIONS
AND MUSTARD

PORK, ROTKOHL
& BACON SPAETZLE

ACCOMPANIED
WITH PRETZEL
& RYE ROLLS

Desserts

APPLE STRUDEL

BLACK FOREST CAKE

Oktoberfest Recipes

Courtesy of Shay and Brian Geyer

GERMAN WALDORF SALAD

Serves 6

4 large Red Delicious apples

1 lemon, juiced

1 medium-sized celery root

½ cup mayonnaise

¼ cup sour cream

4 tablespoons apple cider vinegar

1 tablespoon fresh chopped dill

1 tablespoon fresh chopped parsley

Salt and black pepper to taste

1½ cups walnuts, chopped

Directions

Peel apples, remove cores, and slice or cube. Drip some lemon juice over the apples to keep them from turning brown. Peel and grate the celery root and set aside. In a large salad bowl, mix mayonnaise, sour cream, apple cider vinegar, dill, parsley, salt, and black pepper to taste. Combine grated celery root and dressing, and mix gently. Let sit 20–30 minutes. Add apples and walnuts. Mix well. Garnish with chopped parsley.

GLUHWEIN (HOT GERMAN SPICED WINE)

Serves 6

2 medium lemons

2 medium oranges

10 whole cloves

5 cardamom pods

1¼ cups granulated sugar

1¼ cups water

2 3-inch cinnamon sticks

2 750-milliliter bottles dry red wine such as Cabernet Sauvignon

½ cup brandy

Cheesecloth

Butcher's twine

Directions

Using a vegetable peeler, remove the zest from the lemons and oranges in wide strips, avoiding the white pith; place the zest in a large saucepan. Juice the lemons and oranges and add the juice to the pan. Place the cloves and cardamom in a small piece of cheesecloth, tie it tightly with butcher's twine, and add the bundle to the saucepan. Add sugar, water, and cinnamon sticks; place the pan over high heat and bring to a simmer, stirring to dissolve the sugar. Reduce heat to low and continue to simmer, stirring occasionally, until the mixture is reduced by a third, about 20 minutes. Add the red wine and brandy, stir to combine, and bring just to a simmer (don't let it boil). Remove from heat and discard the spice bundle before serving.

BAVARIAN BEER–ROASTED PORK

Serves 6

3½ pounds pork shoulder, boned and scored

10 cloves, ground in a mortar

2 heaping teaspoons salt

1 pint beer

3 medium-sized onions, quartered

2 sweet potatoes, cubed

3 parsnips, cubed

1 cinnamon stick, broken into 3 pieces

3 star anise pieces (optional)

2 tablespoons mustard seeds

Gravy

8 ounces chicken broth

1 tablespoon elder flower jelly, plus more to taste

½ teaspoon Dijon mustard, plus more to taste

Pepper to taste

Directions

Preheat oven to 350 degrees. Mix the cloves with the salt and rub into the scored pork rind. Put the meat on a deep tray, skin side up, and roast for 1½ hours. Take the tray out, pour the beer over the pork, and arrange the vegetables and spices on the sides. Cook for another 30–45 minutes until the crackling is crisp.

Take out the vegetables and pork and make a gravy in the tray with the broth, jelly, and mustard; season with salt and pepper to taste. Take out the cinnamon stick and star anise and pour into a gravy boat. You can cook it down in a saucepan for a few minutes if you prefer a more concentrated taste. Serve with the meat and vegetables. If the rind isn't crisp enough yet, turn on the grill for a few minutes after you've removed the vegetables, gravy, and spices; cook the meat until the crackling is light and crispy.

PRETZEL BITES WITH BEER CHEESE SAUCE

Serves 6

Pretzels

1½ cups warm water

2 tablespoons light brown sugar

1 package active dry yeast (2¼ teaspoons)

3 ounces unsalted butter, melted

2½ teaspoons kosher salt

4½–5 cups all-purpose flour

1 tablespoon vegetable oil

3 quarts water

½ cup baking soda (for boiling the pretzels)

1 whole egg, beaten with 1 tablespoon cold water

Coarse sea salt

Beer Cheese Sauce

2 tablespoons unsalted butter

2½ tablespoons all-purpose flour

½ cup milk

¾ cup beer

1½ teaspoons Worcestershire sauce

½ teaspoon mustard powder

½ teaspoon garlic powder

2 cups grated sharp cheddar cheese

Pinch of salt and black pepper

Directions

For the pretzels: Combine the warm water, brown sugar, yeast, and butter in the bowl of a stand mixer and mix with the dough hook until combined. Let sit 5 minutes. Add the salt and flour and mix on low speed until combined. Increase the speed to medium and continue kneading until the dough is smooth and begins to pull away

from the side of the bowl, 3–4 minutes. If the dough seems too wet, add more flour, a tablespoon at a time. Remove the dough from the bowl, place on a flat surface, and knead into a ball with your hands. Oil a bowl with vegetable oil, add the dough, and turn to coat with the oil. Cover with plastic wrap and place in a warm spot until the dough doubles in size, about an hour. Preheat the oven to 425 degrees.

Bring 3 quarts water to a boil in a small roasting pan and carefully add the baking soda. It will boil over if not added slowly and cautiously. Remove the dough from the bowl and place on a flat surface. Divide the dough into 8 equal pieces. Roll each piece into a long rope measuring about 24 inches. Cut the dough into 1-inch pieces to make the pretzel bites. Boil the pretzel bites in the water solution in batches, 12–15 at a time, for about 30 seconds. Remove with a large slotted spoon. Place pretzel bites on a baking sheet sprayed with cooking spray. Make sure they are not touching. Brush the tops with the egg wash and season liberally with the coarse sea salt. Place into the oven and bake 15–18 minutes until golden brown. Remove to a baking rack and let rest 5 minutes before eating.

To make the cheese sauce: Melt the butter in a saucepan over medium heat. Add the flour and whisk until you have a paste-like substance, about 1 minute. Add the milk, beer, and Worcestershire, stirring continuously. Add mustard and garlic powder and continue to cook until the mixture thickens, about 5 minutes. Adjust to low heat and stir in the cheddar cheese until smooth and the cheese is melted. Season with salt and pepper.

SAUERKRAUT AND ONIONS

Serves 6

6 slices bacon, chopped

1 large white onion, sliced

1 32-ounce jar or package sauerkraut, drained and rinsed

8 ounces water

1 teaspoon caraway seeds

1 large potato, grated

12 peppercorns

Directions

In skillet, brown onion and bacon. Add sauerkraut, water, caraway seeds, potato, and peppercorns. Simmer for at least an hour. If mixture starts to dry out, add water.

BLACK FOREST CAKE WITH CHERRIES

Serves 6

Cake

1 cup unsweetened cocoa powder

2 cups cake flour

2 cups sugar

2 teaspoons baking powder

½ teaspoon baking soda

1 teaspoon salt

2 cups buttermilk

½ cup vegetable oil

4 large eggs

½ cup dark chocolate chips, melted

Directions

Preheat the oven to 350 degrees. Grease two 9-inch round cake pans with butter or nonstick spray and line with parchment paper. Set aside. In a large mixing bowl, combine the cocoa powder, flour, sugar, baking powder, baking soda, and salt. In a separate bowl, whisk together the buttermilk, oil, and eggs. Gradually beat the wet ingredients into the dry ingredients. Stir in the melted chocolate chips and blend well. Divide the batter evenly between the two prepared round pans. Bake the cakes until a tester comes out clean, 35–40 minutes. Cool the cakes in the pans for 15 minutes, then carefully turn them out onto wire cooling racks to cool completely. Chill in refrigerator 10–15 minutes.

Filling and Frosting

12-ounce jar Morello (sour) cherries

3 cups heavy whipping cream

½ cup powdered sugar

2 tablespoons cherry juice (from the jar)

1 cup grated dark chocolate

Fresh cherries for garnish

To fill and decorate the cake: Remove the cherries from the syrup and set aside both the cherries and syrup. Make the whipped cream. Pour the heavy whipping cream into a large mixing bowl. Start at low speed, gradually increasing to high, adding the powdered sugar and cherry juice as you mix. Beat on high until stiff peaks form, then set aside.

Use a long, serrated knife or cake leveler to cut each round cake in half horizontally. Place the first layer on a cake plate and brush a coating of cherry syrup over the surface. Spread a layer of whipped cream onto the cake and top with a third of the cherries. Repeat with the remaining layers.

Use the rest of the whipped cream to coat the sides and top of the cake. Decorate with the grated dark chocolate and top with fresh cherries. Refrigerate until ready to serve.

Thanksgiving at the Governor's Mansion

Thanksgiving is one of my most treasured holidays. It brings a sense of warmth and grounds us as we think about all we have to be grateful for. As we say grace, pass the numerous high-calorie dishes, and celebrate a day of fellowship, it seems to focus us for the year ahead.

It was a great honor to design this Thanksgiving event at the Arkansas Governor's Mansion. As noted in the Easter Brunch chapter, the State Dining Room is rich in history, since it has been the setting of many state dinners, brunches, and dignitary gatherings.

We incorporated many of the mansion's treasures so you can see precisely how stunning they are. I adore the official state china, which was designed especially for the Governor's Mansion by former Arkansas first lady Janet Huckabee. Members of the Governor's Mansion Association purchased the china as a gift and had commemorative details incorporated into the design. For example, the blue-and-gold rim of each piece is adorned with twenty-five diamonds to represent Arkansas as the twenty-fifth state admitted to the Union in 1836 and to highlight Arkansas's distinction as the only state in North America with a diamond mine in operation. The interior rim contains seventy-five gold barrels representing the state's seventy-five counties, while apple blossoms recall the state flower. Last but certainly not least, the Arkansas State Seal is incorporated and prominently featured. I grounded the state china with gorgeous gold, scalloped Fez Placemats by Kim Seybert.

TIP

I love when napkins serve double duty, here as a place card. They are made from a beautiful African leopard print fabric from Thibaut and tied with a blue velvet ribbon and name card. I embellished them with sprigs of boxwood.

◆ ◆ ◆

Cherished Silver

A portion of the sixty-two-piece silver set from the battleship USS *Arkansas* is proudly displayed in the
dining room's Chippendale-style cabinet. I am sentimental about historic pieces, and it seemed fitting to
make the silver the main attraction for our Thanksgiving festivities. Our florist used some of the silver
as containers for the arrangements. I particularly adore the punch bowl, which perfectly displayed our
centerpiece. Just as the state china contains symbolic elements, the punch bowl is embellished with the
Arkansas State Seal, a sketch of state Capitol buildings, a map outline of the state's counties, apple blossoms,
and eagles. It is rich with historical relevance. Tanarah's Luxe Floral provided an opulent combination of
orange roses, sunflowers, rosehips, and snapdragons with a splash of foraged greenery.

Amazing Grace

After saying grace, guests were treated to a feast that included Arkansas first lady Susan Hutchinson's family recipes, mansion executive chef Daniel Darrah's incredible duck confit crepes, and chef Don Bingham's Thanksgiving fare. One of my favorite beverages is the first lady's famous iced tea. I think my husband was more excited about getting this recipe than any other in the book. It is the best we've ever had.

"*Thanksgiving is a time for counting our blessings of family, friends, and the providential founding of our country.*"

—Arkansas First Lady Susan Hutchinson

A glorious combination of foraged greens, sunflowers, roses, and snapdragons rests on the State Dining Room mantel against the chinoiserie-inspired, hand-painted silk Paul Montgomery wall covering. The wall covering features Arkansas birds and other items of significance to the state. This was one of the components of the dining room I most cherished having the opportunity to design. The first lady weighed in heavily with her vast knowledge of our feathered friends. It took many months of strike-offs to achieve the appropriate scale before production could begin.

FUN FACT

A carpet runner in the Grand Hall bears a variety of state symbols and the names of all twelve governors who have served since 1950. Eleven of the twelve have actually lived in the house.

Appetizer
First Lady's Deviled Eggs

Entrée
Turkey and Dried Fruit Stuffing
with Mansion Cranberry Relish
Grated Zucchini • Sweet and Sour Onions
First Lady's Sweet Potatoe Souflee

Dessert
First Lady's Georgian Pecan Pie
Fruit with Orange Sabayon Sauce

First Lady's Southern Ice Tea
Holiday Bran Rolls

Menu

Thanksgiving Recipes

Courtesy of Chef Daniel Darrah, Arkansas Governor's Mansion

DUCK CONFIT CREPES WITH APPLE-CARDAMOM CRÈME FRAICHE AND BLACKBERRY PORT REDUCTION

Serves 6

1½ pounds cooked duck or chicken (boneless)

6 ounces chanterelle mushrooms, julienned

1 tablespoon duck or chicken fat, or butter

2 cups port wine

2 cups fresh blackberries

2 tablespoons simple syrup

2 ounces fresh basil, julienned

¾ cup Apple-Cardamom Crème Fraiche

Salt and pepper to taste

Directions

Sauté the chanterelles in the duck fat until nicely browned. Add the duck to the pan and toss. Lightly season with salt and pepper. After duck has just begun to steam, toss again and let sit for 30 seconds to allow it to caramelize. Remove from the pan and set aside. While the pan is away from the flame, add the port wine and return to the stove. Bring to a simmer to deglaze and allow the alcohol to burn off. Add the simple syrup. When the edge of the pan starts to bubble, add the blackberries. Swizzle 30 seconds and turn off the heat. While it's cooling, roll the crepes with the duck and mushroom mix. To serve, drizzle crème fraiche across the plate as wide as a pencil. Place the crepes on top and spoon the blackberry sauce across them.

Crepes

1 cup all-purpose flour

1 teaspoon salt

6 eggs

1 cup milk

1 tablespoon orange zest

3 tablespoons clarified butter

Directions

Whisk together flour, salt, and eggs.

Gradually whisk in milk and orange zest. Strain through a sieve and then whisk in the butter. Cover with plastic wrap and let the mixture rest 30 minutes. Place a 5½-inch nonstick pan over medium heat with a teaspoon of butter. Add one ounce of the batter and spread evenly across the pan. Cook until set and flip. The crepe will have a light brown color. Do not overcook. When finished, place on parchment paper.

Apple-Cardamom Crème Fraiche

1 cup whipping cream

2 tablespoons buttermilk

4 cardamom pods

2 cups apple juice

¼ cup dark brown sugar

Directions

Combine whipping cream and buttermilk in a glass container. Cover and let stand at room temperature 8–24 hours, or until very thick. Stir well before covering. When you are ready to create the entire dish, place the apple juice, cardamom, and brown sugar in a pan and reduce over low heat until it has a syrup consistency. Allow to cool to room temperature and stir into the crème fraiche.

ARTISAN WEDGE SALAD WITH BACON-BALSAMIC DRESSING AND TOMATO RELISH

Serves 6

Bacon-Balsamic Dressing

5 slices bacon, ½-inch dice

1 tablespoon minced garlic

5 tablespoons olive oil (optional)

3 tablespoons minced shallots

½ cup balsamic vinegar

1 tablespoon brown sugar

1 tablespoon fresh thyme

Salt and pepper to taste

Sauté the bacon in a pan over medium heat until it is fully cooked. Add the garlic and stir. As soon as the garlic starts to brown, add olive oil and shallots. After a few good stirs, add the balsamic vinegar and deglaze the pan. Add the brown sugar and cook until it has fully dissolved into the liquid. Bring to a boil, then turn off the heat. Allow the dressing to cool for a few minutes. While it is cooling, chop the thyme and then add it to the dressing. Keep warm until service. This can be made in advance and then reheated when the salad is ready to serve.

Relish

2 tomatoes

1 small red onion

2 tablespoons fresh cilantro, minced

2 tablespoons olive oil

2 tablespoons rice wine vinegar or apple cider vinegar

Salt and pepper to taste

1 head artisan leaf lettuce

1–2 tablespoons crumbled feta

Cut the tomatoes in half and remove the seeds. Dice the tomato and onion and place into a mixing bowl. Add the cilantro, olive oil, vinegar, and a pinch of salt and pepper. Stir. Refrigerate at least 30 minutes, then taste. Add more salt, pepper, or vinegar as needed. Pull apart lettuce and place a handful on each plate. Top with relish, dressing, and feta.

Recipes Courtesy of Arkansas First Lady Mrs. Susan Hutchinson

FIRST LADY'S SWEET POTATO SOUFFLÉ

Serves 6

4 large cooked sweet potatoes

1 cup brown sugar

¾ cup pecan halves

2 eggs

1 stick butter

1 cup milk or ½ cup cream

Toppings

¼–½ cup melted butter

1 cup brown sugar

¾ cup pecan halves

OR

Marshmallows

Preheat oven to 350 degrees. Scrub potatoes. Cover with water and cook until tender. Remove from water and allow to cool enough to handle. Slide off the peel and remove any imperfections. Mash in large bowl. Add butter (melt if necessary) and then remaining ingredients. Place in a greased 2-quart baking dish. Bake 30 minutes or until center is stable.

Two topping choices:

1. Remove from oven and top with enough marshmallows to cover. Return to oven and heat until marshmallows melt and are slightly browned. 2. Top with a mixture of melted butter, dark brown sugar, and chopped pecans. Return soufflé to oven and heat another 5 minutes.

FIRST LADY'S GEORGIA PECAN PIE

Serves 6

4 eggs, beaten

1⅓ cups heavily packed dark brown sugar

1⅓ cups light Karo syrup

1⅓ cups unbroken pecan halves

Preheat oven to 425 degrees. Mix ingredients in the order listed. Pour into 9-inch unbaked pie shell. Protect edges of shell with aluminum foil or pie shields. Bake in preheated 425-degree oven for 10 minutes; reduce temperature to 350 degrees and bake another 50 minutes or until a table knife blade comes out clean when inserted halfway to the center of the pie. Remove from oven (center will still be jiggly). Cool and refrigerate before cutting

FIRST LADY'S DEVILED EGGS

Serves 6

6 hardboiled eggs, shelled and sliced lengthwise

1½ tablespoons mayonnaise

1 teaspoon mustard

1 tablespoon sweet pickle relish

Remove yolks and smash. Mix mayonnaise and mustard in a mixing bowl. Add sweet pickle relish. Place mixture back into depressions of egg halves. Garnish yolk with paprika, if desired.

FIRST LADY'S SOUTHERN SWEET ICED TEA

Serves 6

1 tablespoon loose tea leaves

½ teaspoon baking soda

1½ cups sugar

Approximately 1 gallon cool water

Place tea leaves in a small pot with cold water to cover tea leaves. Bring water and tea leaf mixture to a boil, then immediately remove from heat. Sprinkle baking soda over the hot water mixture. Cover and set aside to steep for at least 10 minutes. (Brew may steep longer provided the brew is still warm when you strain into the sugar.) Strain brew through a coffee filter into a pitcher with sugar, stir to dissolve, and continue to add more water from leaf mixture until water runs clear. To serve immediately, add ice cubes until cubes no longer melt and fill with cool water to make a full gallon. The tea is now ready to serve.

Personal note: Only prechilled tea should be served over ice or the full flavor of the tea will be compromised. Allow tea to cool completely before adding additional water or pouring over ice for iced tea.

Recipes Courtesy of Chef Don Bingham, Retired Arkansas Governor's Mansion Administrator

TURKEY WITH DRIED-FRUIT STUFFING

Serves 6

⅔ cup butter or margarine

¾ cup chopped celery

¾ cup chopped onion

8 cups day-old bread crumbs

2½ cups chopped, unpared apples

1½ chopped dried apricots

1½ teaspoons salt

¾ teaspoon pepper

¾ teaspoon dried thyme

12–14-pound turkey

Preheat oven to 350 degrees. In 5-quart Dutch oven over medium heat, cook celery and onion in butter until tender, stirring occasionally. Add bread cubes, apples, apricots, salt, pepper, and thyme. Remove from heat. Fill the turkey neck and body cavity with fruit stuffing mixture. Fasten neck skin to back with skewers. Tie legs together or tuck in band of skin at tail, if present.

Place turkey breast-side up on rack in large roasting pan. Insert meat thermometer deep into inside thigh muscle. Roast uncovered for 1 hour. Reduce temperature to 325 degrees. Continue roasting 2–4 hours longer or until meat thermometer reaches 180 degrees.

During roasting, spoon off accumulated fat at 30-minute intervals. Transfer turkey to platter; remove skewer or string from legs, if used. Let turkey stand 20 minutes for easier carving. Garnish platter with celery leaves and with celery cut to resemble roses, if desired.

HEAVENLY CRANBERRY SAUCE

2 pounds cranberries

2 cups walnuts, coarsely chopped

3 cups sugar

2 lemons, juiced and rinds grated

2 cups orange marmalade

Wash and drain cranberries. Place in shallow baking dish and cover with chopped walnuts, sugar, juice, grated lemon rind, and marmalade. Cover tightly and bake 45 minutes at 350 degrees. Makes 2 quarts.

Winter

Christmas Eve
Dinner and Fellowship

Spend a few minutes with my design pal, Shay Geyer, and you'll fall in love with her vibrant personality. When I discovered she's also an amazing cook, I reached out to see if we could feature her home and cuisine for a Christmas celebration. I was like a kid in a candy store, designing a dinner party in her home. Shay has impeccable taste, so there was a plethora of crystal, napkins, and china to select from. I loved everything she had, so I designed most of the event around her belongings. Shay's also a designer and it was important to me that this chapter represent her brand as well as mine. We decided to steer away from the expected and layer the table in a beautiful shade of pink that paired nicely with her vibrant home and textiles.

TIP

Create an ambient glow by incorporating colored, tapered candles with your tablescape.

◆ ◆ ◆

Pretty in Pink

We created an elegant yet unexpected tablescape by incorporating a combination of
pink, blue, and emerald. Shay's blue Waterford glasses in the classic Lismore pattern
were striking against our nontraditional florals, which included pink sweet peas, Pink
Floyd roses, red anemones, and holiday greenery.

Set the Scene

No event is complete without a well-set table. I paired Shay's blue-and-emerald Mottahedeh Malachite dinnerware with Sparkle Home's rhinestone chargers to create holiday glamour.

Lush magnolia garland from Weston Farm was draped over the mantel and filled with ribbon, peacock feathers, and fresh floral.

Weston Farm's luxurious magnolia wreaths and garland are the brainchild of Erin Weston from Garner, North Carolina. Since establishing the magnolia farm of more than 10,000 trees in 2002, Erin's product has graced the pages of publications such as *House Beautiful*, *Garden and Gun*, *Southern Living*, and *Architectural Digest*.

TIP

Pair bold color with neutrals for maximum impact.

TIP

Incorporate fresh garland for an authentic appeal.

"Every good and perfect gift is from above, coming down from the Father of the heavenly lights, who does not change like shifting shadows." —James 1:17

Dress to Impress

When I'm the host, I like to dress in clothing that coordinates with the overall design. I saw immediately that Shay and I were truly design soul sisters when she arrived in an outfit that went perfectly with our event. Her green taffeta skirt and crisp white shirt, paired with a large-scale necklace, harmonized with the setting.

An Amazing Night of Fellowship

An elegant buffet takes the stress out of entertaining and allows a host to mingle with the guests and enjoy the moment. Fellowship and fabulous cuisine made for a perfect Christmas dinner party. Honey-Roasted Carrots, Geyer Corn Soufflé, and Eggnog Pie were a few of the crowd-pleasers. In these pages, I have provided recipes for a few of her cherished holiday fare for you to share at your next gathering.

Christmas Eve Recipes

Courtesy of Shay and Brian Geyer, IBB Design

HOLIDAY SANGRIA

Serves 6

½ cup agave nectar

¼ cup Grand Marnier

¼ cup brandy

1 large orange, halved and sliced

1 large lime, sliced

1 large green apple, sliced

2 sticks cinnamon

1 bottle good-quality Cabernet

1 can Gosling's ginger beer

Directions

In a large pitcher, add agave nectar, Grand Marnier, brandy, orange, lime, green apple, and cinnamon sticks and stir to combine. Pour in the entire bottle of red wine and stir. Cover and place in the refrigerator for 1–2 hours. Note: The longer it sits, the better it will taste.

Right before serving, add the ginger beer to the sangria mixture. Pour over ice and serve chilled. Garnish with cinnamon sticks and sliced fruit.

BAKED FIGS WITH GOAT CHEESE

Serves 6

Fall is the perfect season for all things fig. Guests love it when Shay serves this simple, beautiful appetizer. When selecting your figs, choose fruit whose stems are a tad bent and whose skin is starting to appear weary. Store figs at room temperature or in the fridge for a couple of days.

6 medium figs

2.8 ounces soft goat cheese

2 tablespoons chopped walnuts

1 tablespoon chopped sage

2 tablespoons honey

Salt and freshly ground black pepper to taste

Directions

Preheat the oven to 400 degrees. Remove the stems and cut an X into the top of each fig halfway through. Using a teaspoon, stuff figs with soft goat cheese. Sprinkle chopped walnuts and sage over the stuffed figs and drizzle with honey. Add salt and freshly ground black pepper to taste. Place in a buttered baking dish. Broil for about 5 minutes or until they look soft and release juice. Serve warm or cold.

DUNGENESS CRAB–STUFFED MUSHROOMS

Serves 6

When traveling the West Coast, Shay and her husband, Brian, enjoy fresh seafood and wine. Shay loves to add Dungeness crab to this mushroom recipe. You can skip the crab and still have a delicious appetizer. It's always a hit.

20 large mushrooms, any variety

½ pound Dungeness crab meat

3 tablespoon olive oil

3 tablespoons butter

3 fresh garlic cloves

3 green onions, chopped

3 tablespoons fresh parsley, finely chopped

2 teaspoons dried oregano

2 teaspoons salt (more to taste)

2 teaspoons freshly ground black pepper

2 cups Italian seasoned bread crumbs

1 cup sherry (or Sauvignon Blanc)

1 cup grated parmesan cheese

1 cup grated fontina cheese

½ cup cream cheese

Directions

Preheat oven to 400 degrees. Clean mushrooms, remove stems, and chop finely. Brush mushroom tops with olive oil. Sauté chopped garlic and green onion in the butter. Add parsley, oregano, chopped mushroom stems, salt, and pepper. Remove from heat, add bread crumbs and ½ cup wine, and mix well. Stir in ¾ cup parmesan, ½ cup fontina, and cream cheese until moist enough to stick together. Add the crab (add more wine if it is dry). Stuff mushroom caps generously and top with the rest of the fontina and parmesan. Place mushrooms in a lightly oiled glass baking dish and pour in remaining wine to make a sauce to drizzle over mushrooms. Bake 15–20 minutes until mushrooms are tender and lightly browned.

GREEN SALAD WITH GORGONZOLA AND RASPBERRY VINAIGRETTE

Serves 6

You can customize this salad with different greens, fruits, cheeses, and nuts. This is Shay's favorite combination.

Raspberry Vinaigrette

4 teaspoons Dijon mustard

½ teaspoon dried oregano

½ teaspoon ground black pepper

1 cup raspberry wine vinegar

1 cup vegetable oil

1 cup white sugar

Directions

Place all ingredients in a jar, shake, and refrigerate overnight.

Salad

1 cup walnuts

1 cup sugar

6 cups mixed spinach and romaine (or other greens)

1 cup red onion, thinly sliced

2 cups pears, thinly sliced

1 cup dried cranberries

1 cup crumbled gorgonzola cheese

Directions

Place walnuts and sugar in a skillet over medium heat, stirring constantly until the sugar dissolves into a light brown liquid and coats the walnuts. Remove walnuts from skillet and spread on a sheet of aluminum foil to cool. In a large bowl, add greens, onion, pears, cranberries, gorgonzola, and walnuts; mix. Dress with refrigerated dressing and serve.

CREAMY MUSHROOM SOUP

Serves 6

You can use any type of mushroom for this recipe. Shay likes to mix cremini, baby bella, and white buttons. Save some mushrooms to pan roast for a pretty topping.

4 leeks

3 tablespoons butter

5 garlic cloves, minced

1½ pounds mixed mushrooms, sliced, any variety

2 teaspoons fresh chopped thyme

4 cups chicken or vegetable stock

1 cup dry white wine

⅓ cup dry sherry

1¼ cup heavy cream

Salt and pepper to taste

Creme fraiche to garnish

Fresh parsley to garnish

Directions

Trim the green ends from leeks. Cut the white ends into quarters lengthwise and thoroughly wash. Chop the leeks into small pieces. Place a large saucepan over medium heat and add butter. Once the butter has melted, add the leek and garlic. Sauté 3–5 minutes, then scoop out and set aside. Add the mushrooms and thyme to the pan. Sauté the mushrooms until the moisture has released and evaporated, about 10 minutes. Then scoop out three-fourths of the mushrooms and set aside. Return the leeks to the pot. Pour in the stock, wine, and sherry. Bring to a boil, then lower the heat. Simmer 15 minutes. Purée the soup, using an immersion blender. Then return the remaining

mushrooms to the pot. Stir in the cream. Season with salt and pepper to taste. Garnish with crème fraiche and parsley.

HONEY-ROASTED CARROTS

Serves 6

2 pounds baby or thin carrots, peeled, tops chopped so that carrots are 2 inches long

¼ cup apricot preserves

2 tablespoons honey

2 tablespoons olive oil

1 tablespoon butter, melted

1 teaspoon balsamic vinegar

1 teaspoon garlic powder

¼ teaspoon ground mustard

¼ teaspoon fresh thyme

⅛ teaspoon ground cumin

¾ teaspoon salt

⅛ teaspoon pepper

Chopped fresh parsley for garnish

Directions

Preheat oven to 375 degrees. Line a baking sheet with foil and lightly spray with nonstick cooking spray (or spray your unlined baking sheet with cooking spray). Add carrots to the center. Set aside. In a medium bowl, whisk together all remaining ingredients and pour over carrots. Toss until evenly coated. Place carrots in a single layer. Bake 30–45 minutes (stirring after 20 minutes), until carrots are fork tender. Roast longer for more caramelization, if desired. Garnish with fresh parsley.

BOURSIN CHEESE MASHED POTATOES

Serves 6

Shay's family loves mashed potatoes, and she likes to get creative with adding flavors. This has become her family's favorite version, and they enjoy them at almost every holiday meal.

8 medium Yukon gold potatoes

1 package garlic-and-herb Boursin cheese

1 cup sour cream

1 stick butter

Salt and pepper

Chopped fresh parsley

Directions

Peel and boil potatoes until fork tender (you can boil them in chicken broth for added flavor). Add cheese, sour cream, and butter to hot potatoes; use a potato masher to mix until smooth and creamy. Add salt and pepper to taste. Garnish with fresh parsley.

GARLIC WINE MUSHROOMS

Serves 6

Mushrooms are a great addition to any beef dish, and these are incredibly simple. Shay serves them as a side dish.

2 tablespoons butter

1 tablespoon olive oil

3 cloves garlic, minced

¼ cup red wine

1 pound mushrooms

2 tablespoons fresh-squeezed lemon juice

2 tablespoons chopped parsley

Directions

Heat butter and olive oil in a skillet over medium heat. When butter is melted and begins to bubble, add garlic, stirring frequently, until it turns just golden, about 30 seconds. Stir in red wine and return mixture to simmer. Add mushrooms and toss to coat. Cover and simmer on medium-low heat for 15 minutes. Remove lid; season with salt and pepper. Continue cooking on medium-low heat for an additional 5–8 minutes, until the mushrooms are cooked through and the bottoms are golden. Drizzle with lemon juice. Garnish with parsley.

MOM'S BEEF TENDERLOIN

Serves 6

Shay's mother has been making this recipe for Christmas dinner since Shay was a child, and it's her absolute favorite. It's easy to make and the flavors are to die for.

4 pounds beef tenderloin

⅓ cup dried rosemary

⅓ cup minced garlic in oil

2 tablespoons seasoning salt

2 tablespoons black pepper

⅓ cup olive oil

¾ cup balsamic vinegar

Directions

Mix rosemary, garlic, seasoning salt, pepper, olive oil, and balsamic vinegar together until well blended. Place this marinade and the tenderloin in a 1-gallon zipper-lock bag and marinate for 24 hours in the refrigerator.

Set the oven to 350 degrees. Remove most of the rosemary and garlic from the tenderloin. Pour 2 tablespoons of olive oil into a large skillet on medium heat. Sear the tenderloin on all sides. Cover lightly with foil and bake the tenderloin to your desired temperature, using a thermometer to determine doneness: rare, 125 degrees; medium, 145 degrees; medium-well, 160 degrees. Remove tenderloin from oven and let rest 10 minutes. Slice and serve on a platter. Top meat with juices from the pan.

MARIONBERRY SHORTBREAD TRIFLE

Serves 4

During the holiday season, Shay likes to serve unusual, yummy treats. On the West Coast, she discovered the marionberry, a cross between Chehalem and Olallie blackberries. Shay says they are better than any other blackberry on the market. If you can't find them, substitute another blackberry or mix a couple of varieties.

½ cup butter, diced

¼ cup powdered sugar

½ cup plus 4 tablespoons granulated sugar

1⅔ cups all-purpose flour

14 ounces blackberries or marionberries (about 3 cups)

1 teaspoon cornstarch

8 ounces mascarpone

1 cup whipping cream

Directions

In a mixing bowl, beat the butter, powdered sugar, ½ cup granulated sugar, and a pinch of salt with the whisk attachment until creamy. Add the flour and knead with your hands to make a smooth dough. Cover and chill for 30 minutes. Place the berries in a saucepan with 2 tablespoons sugar and 5 tablespoons water. Cover and simmer for 2 minutes. Mix cornstarch with a little cold water until smooth and stir into the berry

mixture, simmering for 1 minute. Remove from the heat and allow to cool. Preheat the oven to 325 degrees. Line a baking sheet with parchment.

On a lightly floured work surface, roll out the dough to ⅓-inch thick. Using a 2½-inch pastry cutter, cut 10 circles, rerolling the dough when necessary. Lay on the baking sheet. Bake for 20 minutes, until lightly browned. Allow to cool. Place the mascarpone, cream, and remaining 2 tablespoons sugar in a bowl and beat with the whisk attachment until stiff peaks form. Stir in 4 tablespoons berries to form a swirled effect. Crumble four shortbreads and distribute in four 8-ounce dessert glasses. Spoon half the remaining blackberries over the shortbread, top with the mascarpone cream, then finish with the remaining blackberries. Chill until ready to serve.

Garnish with shaved chocolate for an extra flourish.

EGGNOG PIE

Serves 6

½ 15-ounce package refrigerated pie crust

1 cup sugar

4 large eggs

1 12-ounce can evaporated milk

¾ cup water

¼ cup light rum

⅛ teaspoon salt

½ teaspoon ground nutmeg

¼ teaspoon ground cinnamon

Whipped cream for garnish

Powdered sugar for garnish

Mint for garnish

Directions

Preheat oven to 350 degrees. On a lightly floured surface, unroll pie crust. Roll pastry into a 12-inch circle. Press pie crust into a 9-inch deep-dish pie plate, crimping edges, if desired. Lightly poke holes into the bottom of the dough once it's fitted firmly in the plate. In a large bowl, beat sugar and eggs at medium speed with an electric mixer until well combined. Add evaporated milk, water, rum, and salt. Beat at low speed until combined. Pour mixture into crust. Sprinkle top of pie with nutmeg and cinnamon. Place pie onto a rimmed baking sheet with a depth of ½ inch. Add hot water to baking sheet. Bake for about 55 minutes, or until a wooden pick inserted near the center comes out clean. Cut into desired sizes and garnish with whipped cream, powdered sugar, and mint.

New Year's Eve at Oakmont Estate

W hen I entered the gates of Oakmont Estate, Jim Norton and Robert Walden's Jackson, Tennessee, home, I found myself almost wishing it were spring so I could see the landscape in full bloom. To say it is grand is an understatement. Lush green acres, an abundance of flower beds, and mature trees—I imagine all have stories to tell.

Entering the foyer, we were greeted by the most down-to-earth Southern man I'd ever met. "Come on in, y'all!" Jim beckoned to us as his beautiful, soft-spoken mother took our coats. Jim, host of *The Norton Recipe* cooking show, stood at the foot of the double staircase in jeans and a white tee shirt, impeccably accessorized with a Gucci belt and designer loafers. I love that a person can be both casual and glam. I knew immediately that we were going to have the New Year's Eve of a lifetime.

TIP

Unusual napkin rings make for interesting dinner conversation and act as artwork. Kim Seybert's Fly Away napkin ring is adorned with quartz and brass.

Time, Time, Slipping Away

A mixture of silver and gold is a perfect complement to any New Year's Eve celebration and can be combined with almost any color palette. I incorporated it with traditional black, silver, and cream, while unexpected linen patterns add interest. Thibaut fabric in Laos Beige and Waterford patterns harmonized with the traditional elements in the room. I adored Jim's collection of dinnerware so I decided to delve into his cabinet. I used his silver chargers and topped the table setting with his Mikasa Palatial Gold china and scalloped antique Limoges gold china. As a final detail, I integrated Kim Seybert's Fly Away black-and-gold bee napkin rings, each bee featuring a quartz abdomen and brass wings. With the addition of clocks and pocket watches at each place setting, the guests were able to keep track of time as we looked forward to ringing in the New Year.

TIP

Pocket watches can serve as functional reminders of time, but also as place cards for guests.

◆ ◆ ◆

Ringing in the New Year

After cooking an elegant dinner, Jim entertained his guests around the piano
as they sang their favorite, sentimental songs.

FUN FACT

*Jim and Robert have an extensive collection
of silver champagne buckets. Pictured here is
one of twenty they have collected on travels
throughout the South.*

Jim's menu was rich in flavor and, frankly, blew me away. He isn't a classically trained chef but his skill and talents are vast. I'm not surprised that he has a list of Jackson residents lining up to have dinner at his home. Southern hospitality, a gorgeous estate, and amazing cuisine made our New Year's Affair a night to be remembered.

*"You are never too old to set another
goal or to dream a new dream."*
—*C. S. Lewis*

First Course
PAN SEARED SEA SCALLOPS
ATOP SWEET CORN PURÉE

Second Course
ROASTED CAULIFLOWER BISQUE WITH
GOLDEN RAISINS AND WHITE TRUFFLE OIL

Third Course
PEPPER CRUSTED FILET MIGNON
WITH A RED WINE REDUCTION,
CREAMAYO MASHED POTATOES,
AND SAUTÉED BABY SPINACH WITH
PINE NUTS AND GOLDEN RAISINS

Fourth Course
DECADENT CHOCOLATE TRUFFLE
WITH SWEET RASPBERRY CREME

Happy New Year 2018

New Year's Eve Recipes

Courtesy of Jim Norton of
The Norton Recipe

ROASTED CAULIFLOWER BISQUE WITH GOLDEN RAISINS AND WHITE TRUFFLE OIL

Serves 6

1 medium cauliflower

½ cup plus 2 tablespoons butter

1 large yellow onion

3 ribs celery

2½ cups low-sodium chicken broth

2 chicken bouillon cubes

¾ cup heavy cream

½ teaspoon nutmeg

Salt

Pepper

Cinnamon

Golden raisins

White truffle oil

Preheat oven to 350 degrees. Cut cauliflower into bite-sized florets and place in a baking dish. Melt ½ cup butter and pour over the cauliflower. Toss to coat. Add ½ cup water to the bottom of the dish and tent with aluminum foil. Bake 45 minutes, remove the foil, and bake an additional 10 minutes until slightly brown.

While the cauliflower is baking, chop the onion and celery. In a large skillet over medium-high heat, sauté onion and celery in 2 tablespoons butter until tender. Add 2 cups chicken broth and bouillon cubes. Cook 2–3 minutes and remove from heat. When cauliflower is baked, add it to the onion and celery with the remaining ½ cup chicken broth and return to heat. Cook on medium heat until the cauliflower is tender, 5–6 minutes. Working in batches, purée the mixture in a blender until smooth, and transfer to a medium-size stock pot. Add heavy cream, nutmeg, salt and pepper, and a dash of cinnamon. Stir well. Return to low heat. To serve, ladle bisque into individual bowls. Drizzle with white truffle oil. Garnish with a small handful of golden raisins.

PAN-SEARED SEA SCALLOPS WITH SWEET CORN PURÉE AND TOMATO

Serves 6

24 sea scallops

Salt and pepper

Sweet Corn Purée

1 large shallot, minced

12 ounces fresh or frozen corn

3 teaspoons butter

¾ cup heavy cream

½ teaspoon salt

½ teaspoon black pepper

⅛ teaspoon crushed red pepper flakes

Tomato Garnish

1 cup cherry tomatoes, diced

1 teaspoon fresh parsley, chopped

¼ teaspoon salt

¼ teaspoon black pepper

1 tablespoon olive oil

Corn purée: In a medium skillet, sauté shallot in olive oil until translucent. Add corn (thaw if frozen), butter, and heavy cream. Cook 2 minutes and remove from heat. Add salt, black pepper, and red pepper flakes. Purée in blender until smooth.

Tomato garnish: In a small mixing bowl, add tomatoes, parsley, salt, pepper, and olive oil. Toss to combine.

Scallops: Pat scallops dry with paper towel to remove excess moisture. Season both sides with salt and pepper. In a large skillet, heat a tablespoon of olive oil over medium-high heat. When oil is hot, add half the scallops to the skillet and cook approximately 2½ minutes per side. Do not overcook or the scallops will become rubbery. Remove scallops to a plate and repeat with the remaining scallops.

To serve, place a dollop of the sweet corn purée in the middle of a small, individual plate. Place three scallops on the plate, leaving a small area in the middle of the scallops. Place a spoonful of the tomato mixture in the middle.

BABY SPINACH WITH PINE NUTS AND GOLDEN RAISINS

Serves 6

1 tablespoon olive oil
1 teaspoon minced garlic
¼ cup pine nuts
½ cup golden raisins
2 pounds baby spinach
3 tablespoons butter
Salt and pepper

In a large skillet over medium heat, add oil and garlic and cook for about 2 minutes. Add pine nuts and golden raisins. Toss and cook another minute or so. In batches, add spinach and stir. Cook just until tender, about two minutes. Add butter and salt and pepper to taste.

CREAMAYO MASHED POTATOES

Serves 6

6 medium-large baking potatoes, coarsely chopped, skin on

4 tablespoons butter, room temperature
½ cup sour cream
½ cup mayonnaise
1 heaping tablespoon chives
Salt and pepper

Place chopped potatoes in a medium stock pot and cover with water. Add about ½ tablespoon salt and bring to a boil, covered, 12–15 minutes until tender. Remove from heat and drain. Add butter and sour cream to the potatoes. Mash with a potato masher until well blended. Add mayonnaise and chives. Stir well. Add salt and pepper to taste.

PAN-SEARED PEPPER-CRUSTED FILET MIGNON WITH BEURRE ROUGE (RED BUTTER SAUCE)

Serves 8

8 filet mignons, about 5 ounces each, 1½ inches thick
Salt
Coarse black pepper
Olive oil

Remove filets from refrigerator about 30 minutes before cooking. Generously season both sides of the filets with salt and pepper, patting into the meat. Drizzle olive oil into a large skillet over medium-high heat. When the oil begins to dance, add filets. (You can cook about 4 filets at a time.) Cook filets 3–4 minutes per side for medium-rare. Transfer from skillet to a plate, cover with aluminum foil, and let rest 5 minutes.

Beurre Rouge

1 cup Cabernet Sauvignon
4 tablespoons cold butter, cut into cubes
Pepper

In a small saucepan over medium-high heat, bring red wine to a boil. Reduce to medium heat and simmer for 10 minutes. Remove from heat and add cold butter to the saucepan. Swirl the pan until the butter melts and the sauce thickens. Season with pepper to taste. To serve, place filets on individual plates and spoon sauce over the top of each filet.

DECADENT CHOCOLATE TRUFFLE WITH SWEET RASPBERRY CRÈME

Serves 6

2 cups crumbled chocolate graham crackers
6 tablespoons melted butter
1 cup milk chocolate chips, such as Ghirardelli
2 8-ounce packages cream cheese
½ cup sugar, plus 2 tablespoons
2 eggs
1½ teaspoons vanilla
1 cup frozen raspberries
1 cup heavy cream
Fresh raspberries for garnish

Preheat oven to 350 degrees. Lightly butter the bottom of a 9-inch springform pan. Place chocolate graham cracker crumbs and melted butter in a small mixing bowl. Stir until blended. Press mixture into the bottom of the springform pan. Bake approximately 8 minutes or until crust is set. Remove from the oven and set aside to cool.

In a microwave-safe bowl, melt chocolate chips in 30-second intervals, stirring at each interval until smooth. Set aside. In a large mixing bowl, beat cream cheese and sugar on medium speed until smooth. Add eggs one at a time. Stir in melted chocolate and vanilla. Pour filling into prepared crust.

Bake 35 minutes. The outer rim of the truffle will be firm; however, the middle will jiggle slightly. Remove and cool. Using a knife, loosen the cake from the sides of the springform pan. Remove the sides of the pan. Cover truffle with plastic wrap and chill at least two hours, preferably overnight.

Sweet Raspberry Crème: Place the raspberries in a blender. Add heavy cream and 2 tablespoons sugar. Blend a few seconds, stir, blend again, and stir until the raspberries are puréed. The mixture will be fairly thick. For a thinner sauce, add a bit more cream. To serve, slice the truffle and place on individual plates. Spoon raspberry crème over the top of each piece and garnish with three fresh raspberries.

Valentine's
XOXO
Chic Dinner

R ed is the color most associated with Valentine's Day celebrations. But when I began planning a luxurious Valentine's dinner at the home of my clients, Shirley and Bill Miller, I decided to focus on pink. I opened my Thibaut fabric books and started thumbing through linen options, finally settling on Castera Damask in pale pink as my focal point to begin the design process. Tanarah Haynie, lead designer at Tanarah Luxe Floral, expanded on the theme with stylish, compact floral arrangements that featured roses in multiple tones of pink along with splashes of coral ranunculus.

TIP

When designing floral for a tablescape, use varying shades of the same color for depth.

Belle of the Ball

I often feel like the belle of the ball in the Millers' formal dining room. I gave the room a facelift in 2017, and its lovely neutral canvas has worked well for many special occasions. Our pink Valentine's palette turned out to be exquisite when layered with the room's cream, gold, silver, and champagne tones.

I'm often asked to name the most important element in entertaining. The answer? Selecting a dining table that fits your lifestyle and also the type of entertaining you plan to do. Homeowners are often overwhelmed when selecting a dining table, and for good reason. I suggest you think about how many times you plan to entertain each year, the number of guests you traditionally invite, and what types of events you plan to host. If your events tend to be formal, an oval or rectangular table would work best. If you host small, casual parties, round tables are perfect for intimate gatherings. A good resource for dining-room furniture is the Design Network. They offer many different options and can be found at thedesignnetwork.com.

For the Miller home, I selected a John Richard distressed mirrored table because of its glam appeal. I'm also enamored with its metallic silver finish, which coordinated perfectly with the room.

TIP

Instead of using a napkin ring for your napkin, use it to hold the place card. Our napkins were folded crisply and placed under each dinner plate.

FUN FACT

Redesigning an out-of-date chandelier is easier than one would think. I replaced the cloudy glass pendants hanging from the Millers' fixture with fine crystal in clear and gold. I often replace glass pendants with more than one color of crystal to add depth.

"Once in a while
in the middle of an ordinary life
LOVE
Gives us a fairytale."
   —Unknown

Setting Fancy

I was thrilled that Shirley's Lenox Charleston china complemented our tablescape. With its floral band featuring scrolls and geometric designs, the pale blue, pink, and champagne china looked refined sitting on Kim Seybert Shimmer Capiz place mats. A beautifully wrapped package adorned with ribbon topped off each place setting.

Glamorous Style

Vases and candles are important details. I placed crystal votives and vases along the center of the table, then filled them with large-scale rose heads and candles for a simple elegance that brought the look together. Votive candle holders accented with gold hammered metallic draw the eye to the center of the table.

TIP

Candlelight is key to dinner party ambience. Include different shapes, types, and sizes of votives for drama.

TIP

Light candles no earlier than thirty minutes before your party to avoid melted wax. The manufacturer's recommended candle duration is often incorrect.

A Romantic Affair

Chef Payne Harding from Cache Restaurant in Little Rock, Arkansas, is a genius in the kitchen. For our Valentine's dinner, he presented a menu of refined comfort foods and topped off the evening with scrumptious chocolates.

Valentine's Dinner

Lyonnaise Salad
Shallots
Bacon Lardons
Red Wine Vinegar
Poached Egg
Frisée Lettuce

French Onion Soup
Beef Broth
Gruyère Cheese
Brioche Crouton

Braised Short Rib
Whipped Potato
Carrots
Peas
Braising Jus
Parmigiano-Reggiano
Fresh Herbs

Chocolate Bon Bons
Rosemary Caramel
Peanut Butter
Passion Fruit

Valentine's Recipes
Courtesy of Chef Payne Harding, Cache Restaurant

LYONNAISE SALAD

Serves 6

1 cup shallots, minced
1 cup bacon lardons
½ cup red wine vinegar
1 tablespoon butter
6 poached eggs
Salt and pepper to taste
1 bunch frisée lettuce or baby arugula

Directions

Sweat shallots until translucent. Add bacon lardons and cook until tender. Add red wine vinegar and reduce slightly to a syrup. Add a pinch of butter and melt. In a separate pot, poach eggs in 1 quart of water and 1 ounce of white vinegar until soft boil is achieved. Toss lettuce into the vinegar and bacon mixture and divide into six bowls. Top with poached egg; add cracked pepper and salt to taste.

FRENCH ONION SOUP

Serves 6

6 white onions, sliced
2 ounces bacon fat
4 garlic cloves
1 bunch thyme
3 quarts beef stock
6 large croutons
10 ounces Gruyere cheese, grated
4 ounces chives
Salt and pepper
Chives for garnish

Directions

Preheat oven to broil. Sweat sliced onions in bacon fat until translucent, add garlic, and keep cooking. Pluck thyme and add to the pan. Add beef broth and reduce. Season with salt and pepper to taste. Place soup in serving bowl and top with croutons and grated cheese. Put soup bowls under a broiler until cheese melts to a golden brown. Remove from broiler, top with chives, and serve.

BRAISED SHORT RIBS

Serves 6

3 pounds short ribs
4 cups flour
4 cups carrots
4 cups onions
4 cups celery
4 cups English peas
1 tablespoon garlic, minced
Handful of fresh thyme
Handful of fresh oregano
6 ounces tomato paste
4 cups red wine
1 quart beef stock
Italian parsley for garnish

Directions

Preheat oven to 250 degrees. Season short ribs aggressively with salt and pepper. Dust short ribs in flour and pat dry. In an oven-safe pan, sear on the stove top at a high temperature on both sides. Add carrots, onions, and celery, and cook until tender. Add garlic, fresh herbs, and tomato paste. Add red wine and simmer until reduced by half. Add beef stock and return the short ribs to pan. Cover with foil, place in oven, and braise for about 5 hours until extremely tender. Plate ribs with carrots. Cook peas in salted water separately; add peas to plate. Reduce a portion of the braising liquid in a saucepan; add a pinch of butter before plating and check for seasoning. Serve over whipped potatoes and garnish with Italian parsley.

WHIPPED POTATOES

Serves 6

10 russet potatoes, peeled and cubed
1 cup butter
2 cups heavy cream
1 teaspoon white pepper
Salt to taste

Directions

Boil potatoes until tender. Mash potatoes in a mixing bowl. Fold in butter and heavy cream and whip with hand mixer. Season with white pepper and salt to taste.

Winter Wonderland
All That Glitters

Winter soirees call for the elegance of fine crystal, china, and floral. Nothing makes me happier than to set the table on a cold, snowy day and to hear pots and pans clanging in the kitchen as the aroma of dinner fills the air. The week of our Winter Wonderland event, it snowed heavily and I was worried we wouldn't make it to our destination in Tennessee. Fortunately, the melting began and we were able to get on the road.

Jim Norton and Robert Walden's Oakmont Estate served as a perfect "palace" for this affair. With the addition of Posh Floral's stunning arrangements, our gathering had the excitement of a snowy day. White roses, hydrangeas, and peonies intermingled with translucent, pale-turquoise glass balls for a magical effect.

TIP

For a grand winter tablescape, mix permanent snow-covered garland with fresh floral. Add glass balls for radiance and dimension.

Striking Gold

I love gold, and most of my designs include a highlight or two. For our winter wonderland, I integrated both silver and gold into the tablescape. Kim Seybert's Geode napkin rings in gold and acrylic looked mystical paired with Jim's turquoise Mottahedeh Syracuse china atop Arte Italica Vetro silver chargers.

TIP

Ornate silver frames adorned with rhinestones serve as place cards. The guests' names were written in calligraphy for a formal touch.

TIP

For formal dinner parties, miniature salt and pepper shakers should be provided at each place setting.

All That Glitters

Crystal comes in as my second favorite design element. Perhaps that accounts for my reputation for Southern glam and all things that glitter. John Richard crystal obelisks in varying heights occupied the center of the table, providing multiple points of interest and drawing the eye upward. Angie Strange of Posh Floral integrated gold resin deer shed (antlers) throughout the garland for dimension. I added glass turquoise balls to finish the design and bring iridescence to the center of the table.

TIP

Adding metallic resin or natural deer shed to an elegant tablescape lends a polished, organic feel.

TIP

Organza napkins are glamorous and work well for an elegant soiree. However, they are not functional. I tend to place them for table presentation only and replace them with functional napkins in my color palette after guests find their seats.

"He who marvels at the beauty of the world in summer will find equal cause for wonder and admiration in winter."

—John Burroughs

Multiple levels of floral and crystal grace the table. Chiffon napkins at each
place setting add an air of opulence.

Embroidered linens manufactured from Thibaut's Sir Thomas fabric lend a
regal appearance to our table.

First Course
Mascarpone Grits with Country Ham, topped with Filet of Halibut and Mushroom Marsala Broth

Second Course
Mixed Greens Salad with Granny Smith Apple, Red Onion, Dried Cranberries, and Crumbled Feta with Raspberry Vinaigrette

Third Course
Prosciutto Wrapped Pork Tenderloin with Caramelized Shallots, Creamy Mushroom Risotto, and Roasted Brussels Sprouts with Bacon

Fourth Course
Goat Cheese Buttercream in Phyllo with Cinnamon Poached Cherries and Candied Pecans

Winter Wonderland Recipes

Courtesy of Jim Norton,
The Norton Recipe

MIXED GREEN SALAD WITH BLACKBERRIES AND SWEET BLUSH VINAIGRETTE

Serves 6

Sweet Blush Vinaigrette

⅔ cup sugar

⅔ cup canola oil

½ cup red wine vinegar

2 teaspoons fresh lemon juice

¼ teaspoon salt

¼ teaspoon pepper

⅛ teaspoon garlic powder

Directions

Place all ingredients in a small mixing bowl and whisk until well blended.

Salad

5 ounces mixed greens, such as green leaf, red leaf, romaine, baby spinach

1 large Granny Smith apple, skin on, cubed and drizzled with lemon juice to prevent discoloring

1 medium red onion, thinly sliced

¾ cup fresh blackberries

6 ounces crumbled feta

1 cup coarsely chopped candied pecans

Directions

In a large mixing bowl, gently toss greens, apple, red onion, blackberries, and feta. Place salad on individual salad plates, top with candied pecans, and drizzle with Sweet Blush Vinaigrette.

PROSCIUTTO-WRAPPED PORK TENDERLOIN WITH BUTTERED SHALLOTS

Serves 6

3 1.15-pound peppercorn pork tenderloins

18 slices prosciutto

7 tablespoons unsalted butter, divided

6 shallots

¼ cup Sauvignon Blanc

¼ cup low-sodium chicken broth

⅛ teaspoon dried rubbed sage

⅛ teaspoon salt

⅛ teaspoon pepper

Directions

Preheat oven to 325 degrees. Pat each tenderloin dry with a paper towel. Wrap each tenderloin completely with the slices of prosciutto, 4 to 6 slices per tenderloin. Drizzle olive oil into a large skillet over medium-high heat. When the oil is hot, add 1 tablespoon of butter. Allow butter to melt and foam. Place the tenderloins in the skillet and sear on all sides, approximately 3 minutes per side. Place the tenderloins in a baking dish and pour the juice from the skillet over the top of each tenderloin. Cover with foil and bake 30 minutes or until done. While the pork is baking, return skillet to medium heat. Cook the shallots in 4 tablespoons butter for 2–3 minutes. Add wine and broth. Cook an additional 3–5 minutes or until the shallots are tender. Remove from heat and add an additional 2 tablespoons of butter, sage, salt, and pepper. To serve, slice tenderloin into ¾-inch medallions. Place on individual plates and top with buttered shallots.

FILLET OF HALIBUT WITH MASCARPONE GRITS AND MUSHROOM MARSALA BROTH

Serves 6

Broth

4 ounces gourmet mushroom blend (crimini, shitake, oyster)

1 tablespoon chopped shallots

6 tablespoons butter

1 cup marsala wine

¾ cup low-sodium beef broth

¼ cup heavy cream

⅛ teaspoon pepper

Salt

Directions

In a small saucepan, melt 1 tablespoon butter over medium heat. Add shallots and cook until translucent, about 2 minutes. Add the mushrooms along with 4 tablespoons of butter. Cook for 3 minutes. Add marsala wine and beef broth. Bring to a simmer and cook for 3 minutes. Reduce heat to low and add remaining tablespoon of butter. Whisk in heavy cream, pepper, and a pinch of salt. Leave on low heat to keep warm.

Grits

12 ounces country ham

4¼ cups water

1 cup quick grits

¾ teaspoon salt, divided

4 ounces mascarpone

¼ teaspoon pepper

Directions

In a large skillet, cook country ham according to the package. Dice the ham and set aside. In a medium saucepan, bring water to a boil over high heat. Add grits and ¼ teaspoon of salt. Stir continuously until mixture returns to a boil. Reduce heat to low, cover, and cook approximately 8 minutes or until mixture reaches desired thickness. Add mascarpone, diced country ham, pepper, and remaining ½ teaspoon salt. Stir to melt the mascarpone and blend. Keep warm over low heat.

Halibut

Serves 6

8 3–4 ounce fillets of sea bass (about 1½ inches thick)

Salt and pepper

Fresh parsley for garnish

Preheat oven to 350 degrees. Arrange fillets on a baking sheet lined with parchment paper. Season both sides of the fillets with salt and pepper. Bake for approximately 15 minutes or until flaky. The baking time will depend on the thickness of your fish. Remove from oven and prepare to plate.

To serve, spoon a large dollop of the grits mixture into individual shallow bowls. Place a halibut fillet on top of the grits. Spoon the marsala broth with mushrooms over the top of the fillet. Sprinkle with fresh chopped parsley to garnish.

CREAMY MUSHROOM RISOTTO WITH CRUMBLED PROSCIUTTO

Serves 6

4 slices prosciutto

1 tablespoon olive oil

2 tablespoons butter

1 medium yellow onion, diced

1½ cups arborio rice

¾ cup Sauvignon Blanc

6 cups low-sodium chicken stock

¼ cup shredded parmigiano-reggiano

8 ounces sliced baby bella mushrooms

Salt and pepper to taste

Directions

Preheat oven to 350 degrees. Place prosciutto slices on a baking sheet and bake until crispy. In a large stock pot, heat chicken stock over medium heat. While the chicken stock is warming, heat olive oil and butter in a large skillet over medium heat. Sauté diced onion until tender and translucent, 3–4 minutes. Add rice and cook for about 1 minute. Add white wine and stir. Add warm chicken stock to the skillet one ladle at a time. Stir continuously, allowing the rice to absorb all the stock before adding the next ladle. Continue until you've used all the chicken stock. Stir in parmigiano-reggiano, mushrooms, and an additional tablespoon of butter, and cook until mushrooms are tender. Add salt and pepper to taste. Place a scoop of risotto on individual plates and top with crumbled crispy prosciutto.

ROASTED BRUSSELS SPROUTS WITH ONION AND APPLEWOOD-SMOKED BACON

Serves 6

3 pounds brussels sprouts, ends removed and halved

12 ounces applewood-smoked bacon

1 large yellow onion, diced

4 tablespoons butter

1 tablespoon chicken boullion

½ teaspoon pepper

¼ teaspoon crushed red pepper flakes

¼ cup red wine vinegar

Salt and pepper to taste

Preheat oven to 425 degrees. Place brussels sprouts on a baking sheet, drizzle with olive oil, and sprinkle with salt and pepper. Put the brussels sprouts in the oven and bake 20–30 minutes, tossing every 10 minutes. Julienne the bacon. In a skillet, cook over medium heat until done. Remove bacon from skillet and set aside. Using the same skillet containing the bacon grease, sauté onion until translucent, or about 5 minutes. Set heat on low and add roasted sprouts to the skillet with onions. Add butter, chicken bouillon, pepper, crushed red pepper flakes, and red wine vinegar. Stir to combine. Cover and cook over low heat until sprouts are tender, approximately 10 minutes. Add cooked bacon and serve.

GOAT CHEESE BUTTERCREAM IN PHYLLO WITH CINNAMON POACHED CHERRIES AND CANDIED PECANS

Serves 6

Candied Pecans

4 cups pecan halves

½ cup brown sugar

1 cup sugar

2 teaspoons cinnamon

½ teaspoon salt

1 egg white

1 teaspoon vanilla

2 teaspoons water

Drizzle of honey

Preheat oven to 250 degrees and line a

baking sheet with parchment paper. Add brown sugar, white sugar, cinnamon, and salt to a gallon-size plastic bag. Set aside. In a medium mixing bowl, combine egg white, vanilla, water, and honey. Whisk until foamy. Add pecans and toss to coat thoroughly. Place coated pecans into the plastic bag with the sugar mixture. Shake to coat all the pecans. Pour bag of coated pecans onto prepared baking sheet. Bake for 1 hour. Every 15 minutes, stir the pecans on the baking sheet.

Goat Cheese Buttercream

20 ounces goat cheese, softened

1 cup sweetened condensed milk

½ tablespoon vanilla

Place goat cheese, condensed milk, and vanilla in a large mixing bowl. Using a hand mixer, beat on high until well combined and fluffy. Transfer mixture to a pastry bag with a large star tip and store in refrigerator until ready to use.

Phyllo Bowls

½ cup melted butter

10 sheets phyllo dough, thawed

Preheat oven to 350 degrees. Brush a muffin tin lightly with melted butter and side aside.

Unroll phyllo dough (9×14-inch sheets). On a work surface, lay out a single sheet of dough. Brush with melted butter. Place another sheet of phyllo on top and brush with butter. Repeat this step until you have 5–6 layers of phyllo. Cut the stack into 4½-inch squares (you will end up with six squares). Lay each square into a muffin tin, pressing gently to form the shape of the cup. Bake for approximately 15 minutes or until golden brown. Remove from oven and cool completely.

Moscato Cinnamon Cherries

1 pound dark cherries, pitted, fresh or frozen

¼ cup sugar

½ cup moscato wine

1 cinnamon stick

Slice cherries in half. Set aside. In a medium saucepan, add sugar, wine, and the cinnamon stick. Bring to boil over medium-high heat. Turn heat to low and add cherries. Simmer for approximately 5 minutes. Remove from heat. Remove the cinnamon stick and set aside to cool.

Assemble: Fill a phyllo bowl with the goat cheese buttercream from the pastry bag. Spoon some of the moscato cinnamon cherries and syrup over the top. Finish with a few candied pecans.

Shayla Copas

◆ ◆ ◆

Shayla Copas Interiors, Little Rock, Arkansas

Award-winning designer, speaker, author, and philanthropist Shayla Copas is one of the South's most acclaimed luxury designers and tastemakers. She has created innovative interiors for residential, commercial, and event clients during her more than twenty-year career.

Shayla has a reputation as an approachable designer with a natural talent for assessing and addressing her clients' needs. Her firm's rigorous project-intake process ensures that the end result is an accurate reflection of the client's taste, and also that it has the polish only a professional design firm can provide. Shayla Copas Interiors is unparalleled in the industry for the ability to deliver unique projects within the specified time frame and budget.

Shayla describes her design aesthetic as "Southern glam" appeal, with glitz, glamour, pattern, and color as her trademarks. She is often referred to as a color guru because of her keen eye for color, texture, and balance. She loves to add unexpected flourishes to the parties, balls, and gatherings she orchestrates, a trait that has earned her a reputation as a trendsetter. Well known for her event design and entertaining talent, she has executed more than fifty major events, including the Arkansas Inaugural Ball.

In 2015, Arkansas governor Asa Hutchinson appointed Shayla to the Arkansas Governor's Mansion Commission. In that role she worked with the first family on the mansion's renovation. Her firm donated countless hours to the project and was recognized in the 2017 Designer of the Year awards of the Interior Design Society.

Shayla's work has been featured in print regionally and nationally. In fall 2017, she filmed a show called *Southern Glam* with the Design Network, which featured her work. She also appears regularly on *Good Afternoon Arkansas*, where she shares entertaining, design, and lifestyle advice. She can be seen at industry events making trend forecasts, taking part in panel discussions, and participating in Instagram takeovers. Her love of the industry's manufacturers, partners, and fellow designers is contagious, and she makes it a priority to encourage, elevate, and collaborate.

During the course of her career, Shayla has served on numerous nonprofit boards and has been instrumental in raising more than $4 million for a variety of organizations and causes. In 2017, she won the Philanthropist of the Year Award from the Women's Foundation of Arkansas. Shayla works tirelessly to raise funds for her most treasured nonprofits, which focus on the protection and healing of abused children. In 2015, she founded the Woman of Inspiration event for Children's Advocacy Centers of Arkansas to raise money for abuse victims and their families.

Shayla is married to her best friend, Scott Copas, and resides in Little Rock, Arkansas. In her spare time, she loves to entertain and cook for friends and family. A few of her favorite recipes are featured in the Kentucky Derby chapter of this book.

Shayla's design aesthetic has what she calls a "Southern glam" appeal, with glitz, glamour, pattern, and color as her trademarks.

Janet Warlick

• • •

Camera Work Photography, Little Rock, Arkansas

Janet Warlick is an architectural and editorial photographer based in Little Rock, Arkansas. Her work has been featured in national and regional publications highlighting architecture, interior design, and lifestyle. Janet's photos also have been included in several books on travel, tourism, and design.

With a degree in journalism emphasizing photography and art, Janet has distinguished herself in the photography of interior design. Sensitive to nuances of light, she uses photography to interpret three-dimensional spaces in a way that is easily understood and appreciated.

Janet has a passion for the beauty of food photography and enjoys creating mouthwatering images.

Janet's work has been featured in national and regional publications highlighting architecture, interior design, and lifestyle.

Chef Daniel R. R. Darrah

Arkansas Governor's Mansion

◆ ◆ ◆

THANKSGIVING

Daniel Darrah has been cooking professionally for twenty years, and has been a chef at the Arkansas Governor's Mansion since 2015. Daniel not only creates culinary delights for Arkansas's first family, but also for the people who attend the various events, parties, holiday gatherings, and private functions at the mansion.

Originally from San Diego, California, Daniel moved to Georgia in 1999. He began his career working two full-time jobs in the chain restaurant industry and quickly moved up the ranks. However, he didn't feel like he was really cooking, simply assembling food on plates. Working from standardized recipes and boiling things in bags wasn't how he pictured being a chef. Still, the environment was fastpaced, everchanging, and full of excitement. Daniel knew the kitchen was where he belonged. While working at a private golf course in Georgia, he got a glimpse of what a chef's life could be, and he wanted every part of it. After a year, Daniel enrolled in culinary school.

After completing the curriculum, Daniel did an externship at Pebble Beach Golf Resort in California. Within a week he was teaching the cooks better efficiency in their respective workplaces, so the executive chef gave him a cooking test. Daniel had three hours to create two breakfast dishes, two lunch dishes, two entrees, an appetizer, a salad, and a dessert. He succeeded in impressing the chef and was offered a personal chef position for a visiting family. That family hailed from Arkansas.

A year after completing his externship, Daniel received a phone call from the gentleman he cooked for in Pebble Beach, letting him know of an open chef position at a new golf course being built in Arkansas called the Alotian Club. He took the position and worked there for eight years before accepting the chef job at the Governor's Mansion.

While working at a private golf course in Georgia, he got a glimpse of what a chef's life could be, and he wanted every part of it.

Arkansas First Lady Susan Hutchinson

Arkansas Governor's Mansion

◆ ◆ ◆

THANKSGIVING

First Lady Susan Hutchinson brings to the Governor's Mansion a lifetime of experience working to improve the lives of children.

Before assuming the role of first lady when husband Asa Hutchinson became governor, the former schoolteacher spent several years on the board of the Children's Advocacy Center of Benton County, one of sixteen nonprofit Children's Advocacy Centers in the state that work with abused children. Among other initiatives, Susan is working to establish more Children's Advocacy Centers throughout Arkansas.

Susan also hopes to inspire educators to incorporate music into students' daily lives. She believes every child should have the chance to learn to play a musical instrument in school—at least for one year. Susan sees the arts as "brain builders" and hopes to advocate for children's exposure to the arts in general.

Among the organizations Susan supports are the Arkansas Symphony Orchestra, Museum of Discovery, and Arkansas Children's Hospital. In the past, she served on regional boards of the American Heart Association and the Alzheimer's Foundation of America.

A native of Atlanta, Georgia, Susan says she grew up "as blue-collar as you can get" as the second of seven children. She was the valedictorian of Fulton High School with aspirations of being a doctor. Instead, after graduation from Bob Jones University in South Carolina, she taught biology and algebra in Memphis, Tennessee.

The governor and first lady have been married for forty-five years. They have four children, six grandchildren, and a twelve-year-old rescue cat named Snowflake.

Susan hopes to inspire educators to incorporate music into the daily lives of students.

Shay and Brian Geyer

IBB Design, Dallas, Texas

• • •

CHRISTMAS
&
OKTOBERFEST

Shay and Brian spent much of their first year of dating cooking together at each other's homes. Their love of cooking and entertaining continues today, and they're known for hosting fun-filled parties for friends and family. The couple has an extensive collection of favorite family recipes, but they love experimenting with new dishes and putting their own spin on things. Shay refers to Brian as "Grill Master" and "King of the Green Egg."

On any given day, you'll find them in the kitchen cooking with their two daughters, accompanied by their three dogs.

A winner of Fashion Group International of Dallas's Rising Star in Interior Design award, Shay is inspired by fashion, traveling, the arts, family, and friends. She loves every aspect of entertaining, from creating an inviting interior that functions for frequent get-togethers, to planning menus and designing tablescapes full of color, pattern, and texture.

Shay's vibrant personality and personal design approach often land her high-profile and lifelong clients who also rely on her for lifestyle and entertaining advice.

Since 2006, Shay has been the design expert for WFAA-TV's *Good Morning Texas*. She is the editor of IBB Design's quarterly magazine, *IBB Home*, which is distributed to more than 25,000 households.

The Shay Geyer Collection debuted in September 2017 and includes fabrics, art, permanent botanicals, pillows, and more. Shay was one of five distinguished talents selected to create the Portfolio by Nourison high-end area rug collection.

Dallas-based interior designer Shay Geyer and her husband, Brian, are often found in the kitchen, cooking with their two daughters.

Chef Payne Harding

Cache Restaurant, Little Rock, Arkansas

◆ ◆ ◆

VALENTINE'S
&
UNDER THE SEA

Chef Payne Harding is uncommon in many ways. As executive chef and owner of Cache Restaurant in downtown Little Rock, he created a menu of inventive pairings that include locally sourced ingredients when available. He presides over a state-of-the-art kitchen that's visible to patrons as they savor the menu's offerings.

Payne found his love of food at the age of fifteen, when he first tasted merlot and learned about pairing flavors. His first job was as a busboy at Restaurant 1620 in Little Rock. He went on to attend the University of Central Arkansas in Conway, where he earned his bachelor's degree, followed by graduation from the Culinary Institute of America in Hyde Park, New York. A six-month externship at Le Cirque NY completely changed his insight as a chef.

When his father, Rush Harding, opened Cache in 2014, Payne had only recently graduated from the culinary institute. He initially worked with Chef Matt Cooper, and then with Chef Lee Richardson to organize a dinner the Hardings donated at a live auction at the Easter Seals' Arkansan of the Year event.

A six-month externship at Le Cirque NY completely changed Payne's insight as a chef.

Chef Jamie McAfee

Pine Bluff Country Club, Pine Bluff, Arkansas

◆ ◆ ◆

FALL FEST
&
ELEGANT CABIN

You might say that cooking is in Certified Executive Chef (CEC) Jamie McAfee's blood. McAfee—club manager, executive chef, and food and beverage director at the Pine Bluff Country Club—was introduced to the culinary arts as a child by his father, James McAfee.

The elder McAfee was a US Navy chef who later worked for the Peabody Association, which was linked to the Peabody Hotel, during the 1950s and '60s. Eventually, he landed at the Delta Country Club in McGehee, Arkansas, where he was the manager and chef for thirty-seven years until his death.

Jamie worked his way through the Memphis Culinary Academy, where he graduated at the top of his class in 1985. While attending culinary school, he worked full-time as a manager at the Nike Corporation in Memphis. He also juggled being a husband to his bride, Laurie, and father to his son, Jay, also a chef, and his daughter, Ashley.

After working as a chef at Café Meridian in Memphis, Jamie followed in his father's footsteps and returned to McGehee with his family to assume the same role that his father had at Delta Country Club. He moved to the Pine Bluff Country Club in 2003.

Throughout his career, Jamie has been committed to furthering his skills and continuing his culinary education. He has participated in numerous workshops and seminars in San Francisco, Washington, DC, New Orleans, and Florida. He graduated from Pulaski Tech Culinary School with an associate degree in culinary arts. Currently, he's working to obtain the Certified Culinary Educator (CCE) designation. He is also pursuing certification as a club manager.

Jamie teaches at the Arkansas Culinary School at Pulaski Technical College in Little Rock, where he is on the board of directors. He is board chair of the Arkansas chapter of the American Culinary Federation and is a past president of the Arkansas Hospitality Association.

He was named Arkansas Chef of the Year three times and has won two bronze medals in American Culinary Federation competitions, and two gold, two silver, and two bronze medals in Arkansas Hospitality competitions. He has also been inducted into the American Academy of Chefs.

Jamie has donated considerable time to worthy causes and events such as Southeast Arkansas College of Pine Bluff, the National Kidney Foundation, Arkansas Chef Association fundraisers, the Frank Broyles benefit for Alzheimer's research, the Arts and Science Center of Pine Bluff, and Jefferson Regional Medical Center School of Nursing.

However, no work has touched him more deeply than cooking with colleagues for Hurricane Katrina refugees. He cooked alongside Chef Sam Choy twice at the Five Star Chef Event in Cleveland, Ohio; the event benefits UH Seidman Cancer Center. He has helped raise more than $20 million for local and national charities during his culinary career.

Jamie counts among his friends Choy and the late Chef Paul Prudhomme, both of whom he cooked with on several occasions. He was honored to cook at the *Slate* magazine dinner to celebrate philanthropy, attended by former president Bill Clinton and business moguls Warren Buffett, Bill Gates, and Ted Turner.

Jamie has helped raise more than $20 million for local and national charities during his culinary career.

Chef Tim Morton

RH Catering, Little Rock, Arkansas

◆ ◆ ◆

SPRING REHEARSAL DINNER
&
POOLSIDE SOIREE

Born and raised in Little Rock, Arkansas, Chef Tim Morton has always had an interest in cooking. From age eleven through his teens, Tim worked for his aunt in the restaurant business. He competed in culinary competitions in his junior year at Hall High School, placing second overall, and won first place in the same competition during his senior year.

After graduating from high school, Tim received a full scholarship to the Culinary Arts Institute in Atlanta, Georgia. After working in many high-end restaurants in the metro area, he went on to open his own catering company in 1997.

In 2000, he decided to return home to Little Rock. He worked at Restaurant 1620 as executive chef and general manager until he bought the restaurant in 2012. He sold the restaurant in 2016. In 2017, he started RH Catering and currently spends most of his time catering large events all over central Arkansas.

From age eleven through his teens, Tim worked for his aunt in the restaurant business.

Jim Norton

The Norton Recipe, *Jackson, Tennessee*

◆ ◆ ◆

NEW YEAR'S AFFAIR
&
WINTER WONDERLAND

Jim Norton loves nothing more than having guests at his dining table. Raised in the wine country of Northern California, Jim comes from a long line of great cooks.

During his childhood, most meals in the Norton household were eaten at home around the dining table and prepared by a Southern-born mother who made everything from mac and cheese to beef stew. One of Jim's favorite memories is being in the kitchen with his mother, making Christmas cookies and buttercream frosting. Each summer he spent a lot of time with his grandmother, who was a quintessential Southern cook. Fried chicken, catfish, mashed potatoes, and homemade gravy were the norm.

When he was twenty years old, Jim packed what little he owned and headed to Nashville to chase his dreams. Not knowing a soul in the big city was scary, but he knew he had a purpose. Soon after that he met Robert, his partner of nearly eighteen years. They settled into their dream home in Jackson, Tennessee, and started a wholesale art business that evolved into both interior design and furniture retail. When their businesses took off, Jim was finally able to pursue his first passions—food and entertaining.

For the past ten years, Jim has developed a repertoire of simple food made with few ingredients. He lives in a small town with no specialty grocery stores, so he focuses on using basic ingredients and making them better. He has a gift for knowing which flavors will blend well. He didn't attend culinary school, but his guests would never know it.

For Jim, the key components of entertaining are the food, the presentation, and the host. The food can be created with practice by following recipes, tasting, and trying new things. The presentation is all about making people feel special. He says you don't need the finest crystal: "Just use what you have and show that you have paid extra attention. Your guests will know you spent the time because you care." His advice to the host: "Have fun. Enjoy what you are doing. There is nothing better than seeing family or friends gathered around your table, enjoying a meal you have prepared for them."

When Jim and Robert aren't entertaining, they're busy helping others. Each year Jim chairs a local healthcare foundation's charity gala for nearly 700 guests. From food to decor, Jim focuses on making every detail picture-perfect. The evening before the big gala, Jim and Robert host a patron's party for more than 250 guests.

Jim has come a long way. He entertains bigger than ever, cooks better than ever, and lives life on a grand scale. The filming of his cooking show, *The Norton Recipe*, is the cherry on top of his life.

For Jim, the key components of entertaining are the food, the presentation, and the host.

Chef Janice Provost

Parigi, Dallas, Texas

◆ ◆ ◆

SEERSUCKER SOCIAL

J anice Provost is executive chef and proprietor of Parigi, a well-known Dallas restaurant. Her path to cooking professionally began in 1998 after she left a successful career in sales to attend El Centro Community College Food and Hospitality Institute in Dallas. She landed her first kitchen job at Pargi that same year; three years later, she bought the neighborhood bistro.

Born in Houston, Janice was raised in a family that valued farming and agriculture. She grew up with chickens, geese, ducks, bees, and an appreciation for raising crops. That background has influenced her philosophy as a chef, and she grows many of her own herbs and vegetables at Promise of Peace, a community garden in Dallas.

A self-proclaimed francophile, Janice travelers to France whenever possible. She and her husband love to shop the local markets and enjoy cooking in their Paris apartment. They also appreciate the multicultural cuisine for which Paris is known, and many of these dishes find their way back to the menu at Parigi.

A pioneer in the local food movement, Janice supports Texas Farmers and Ranchers and is a member of the Dallas Farmers Market, Friends, and Chef for Farmers, and she serves on the Labajada Garden board of directors.

She created the Parigi Scholarship Endowment Fund, which provides scholarships to students of the El Centro Community College Food and Hospitality Institute. In 2016, Janice received the institute's prestigious Bits and Bites Award for her dedication.

As an advisory board member and past president of the Greater Dallas Restaurant Association (which named her Restaurateur of the Year in 2017) and member of Les Dames d' Escoffier, Janice has helped raise more than $1 million in scholarships for culinary arts students. In 2017, the Texas Restaurant Association named Janice Restaurateur of the Year.

A strong proponent of encouraging women within the industry, Janice is on the advisory board for Letot Girls Residential Treatment Center, where she volunteers as a culinary instructor, teaching students the basics of cooking.

Janice was invited to cook at the James Beard House in New York City in 2014 and 2017. On both occasions, she took along a chef team consisting of her mentors and mentees at Parigi.

One plate at a time, Janice hopes to build a sustainable future through education, mentoring, community, and responsibly sourced food.

▬

A pioneer in the local food movement, Janice supports Texas Farmers and Ranchers.

Chef Scott Rains

Table 28, Little Rock, Arkansas

◆ ◆ ◆

FOURTH OF JULY
&
CINCO DE MAYO

Scott James Rains is a classically trained chef, a restaurateur, and an avid fisherman. Born in Malvern, Arkansas, into a family that loved all things food, he developed a passion for the culinary arts. At nineteen he ventured to San Francisco to embark on his career.

After school, Scott stayed in the Bay Area for more than two decades to hone his craft at multiple Michelin Star restaurants. He speaks fondly of working under Chef Pino Spinoso at Cafe Tiramisu in San Francisco.

Back in Arkansas, his restaurants, Horseshoe Vineyard and Table 28, received praise and awards, including 2014 Top Chef in Little Rock from Little Rock Foodcast. Rains won the University of Arkansas for Medical Sciences Top Bacon Chef title three years running. He is known in the area for his refined palate, unique flavor matching, and pushing the envelope on exotic fare.

Scott works closely with local farmers and gardeners to ensure that his menus speak the language of the land. Table 28 at the Burgundy Hotel is not only his masterwork, but his passion project.

Scott works closely with local farmers and gardeners to ensure that his menus speak the language of the land.

Chef Don Bingham

Retired Administrator
Arkansas Governor's Mansion

◆ ◆ ◆

EASTER BRUNCH
&
THANKSGIVING

Don Bingham retired as the Arkansas Governor's Mansion's administrator after working for two governors, Mike Huckabee and Asa Hutchinson. His culinary skills earned him Arkansas Chef of the Year several years ago. He has appeared on local television shows as a guest chef, including *Good Morning Arkansas* and the *ABCs of Cooking*.

Don has coauthored two cookbooks: *Celebration with Cooking* and *Celebrate the Holidays*. Accomplished across many creative spectrums, Don has recorded four inspirational piano CDs. He is a member of the American Academy Chefs and a class instructor for Arkansas Chefs School.

Don's culinary skills earned him
Arkansas Chef of the Year.

Carmen Portillo

Cocoa Belle Chocolates
Bryant, Arkansas

◆ ◆ ◆

CHOCOLATIER FOR UNDER THE SEA

At age nineteen, Carmen Portillo left her hometown of Little Rock and moved to London, where she had her first handmade chocolate truffle. Later she traveled to Paris and caught chocolate fever. Returning to Little Rock a year later, she longed for that experience again, so she researched ways to learn the artisan truffle trade.

Carmen studied at the Notter School for Confectionary and Chocolate Arts in Orlando, Florida, and received a certificate from Ecole Chocolate Professional Chocolate Arts, making her the first and only certified professional chocolatier in Arkansas.

Cocoa Belle Chocolates specializes in handmade artisan chocolate truffles, barks, sauces, and butters. Her client list for custom work ranges from Fortune 500 companies to government officials.

Recently Cocoa Belle Chocolate landed on the pages of *Vogue's Culinary Collection*, which featured her line of decadent chocolate sauces and chocolate butters.

Carmen is the first and only certified professional chocolatier in Arkansas.

Angie Strange

◆ ◆ ◆

Posh Floral Designs, Dallas, Texas

After more than a decade of designing floral for couture events, Angie Strange, founder of Posh Floral Designs, has become known for her uniquely personal and luxurious creations. Angie is inspired by her clients' styles and aspires to go above and beyond to create designs that are more than they could imagine. She has expanded her business with destination events, which takes her all over the world.

Named one of the Best of the Best Florists in Dallas by *Modern Luxury Magazine*, Posh Floral has designed for numerous entities, among them Chanel, Neiman Marcus, Kendra Scott Jewelry, Mercedes-Benz, Rolls-Royce, Bentley, Zac Posen, Monique Lhuillier, the Dallas Cowboys, David Yurman, and Giorgio Armani.

Whether she's working with a celebrity client or the girl or guy next door, Angie finds joy in creating refined florals for upscale events in Dallas and locations worldwide.

Angie is inspired by her clients' styles and aspires to go above and beyond to create designs that are more than they could imagine.

Dale Aldridge, Tammy Copeland, Brittany Vick

◆ ◆ ◆

Silks A Bloom, Little Rock, Arkansas

Silks A Bloom is a full-service company specializing in holiday, event, and everyday floral design. Its large group of talented professionals is led by Dale Aldridge, Tammy Copeland, and Brittany Vick. Their love of design, impeccable customer service, and wealth of talent has made the company one of the South's top names for floral.

Co-owner Dale Aldridge began focusing on floral design after his high school floriculture team won an Arkansas state title. Brittany Vick learned the business working beside her mother, Tammy Copeland, at the floral studio. The three of them strongly believe in continually evolving and designing outside the box.

Silks A Bloom started out specializing in high-end faux botanicals, then broadened its creative offerings to fresh florals and is now known for its commercial and residential holiday designs. In recent years, the team has also launched a wedding and special-events division.

The company's large commercial commissions have included the Bill and Hillary Clinton National Airport, Marriott Hotels, and Little Rock Convention & Visitors Bureau. However, the design team enjoys catering to any client, no matter how large or small the project. Dale, Tammy, and Brittany believe all projects deserve top-quality design, installation, and service.

Their love of design, impeccable customer service, and wealth of talent has made the company one of the South's top names for floral.

Tanarah Haynie

◆ ◆ ◆

Tanarah Luxe Floral
Little Rock, Arkansas

An award-winning and sought-after floral artist, Tanarah Haynie is the founder and chief creative director of Tanarah Luxe Floral. Her passion for flowers began with picking daffodils at her grandmother's home. She started working in a commercial flower shop at age nineteen and was smitten.

Tanarah's skillful manipulation of botanicals results from an intense study of many disciplines of floral design. After mastering the floral arts, she moved into event design, bringing her vision to transform ordinary spaces with floral compositions.

Since launching her firm in 2000, Tanarah has worked for Fortune 500 companies, nonprofit organizations, and top political leaders and designed events for the Country Music Awards, Paula Deen, Nicole Miller, and the Rolling Stones. Her passion and humble approach to life makes it easy for clients to communicate with her.

Tanarah is an avid educator and a commissioned speaker at floral conferences and shows. She has been featured in *Grace Ormonde Wedding Style*, *Style Me Pretty*, *Southern Bride*, *Southern Living Weddings*, *At Home in Arkansas Weddings*, *Arkansas Bride*, and *Soiree*.

Tanarah's passion for flowers began with picking daffodils at her grandmother's home.

Resources and Credits

• • •

Kentucky Derby

EVENT DESIGN: Shayla Copas (shaylacopas.com)

PHOTOGRAPHER: Janet Warlick, Camera Work Photography (cameraworkphoto.com)

CULINARY CONTRIBUTOR: Shayla Copas (shaylacopas.com)

VENUE: The Pine Hill Ranch (thepinehillranch.com)

VENUE INTERIOR DESIGN: Carrie Kessler

FLORAL: Dale Aldridge, Tammy Copeland, and Brittany Vick of Silks A Bloom (silks-a-bloom.com)

FURNISHINGS AND ACCESSORIES: Park Hill Collection (parkhillcollection.com)

LINEN AND NAPKIN FABRIC: Thibaut (thibautdesign.com)

LINEN SEAMSTRESS: Callie Bullock, Draped and Tailored

CHARGERS: Kim Seybert (kimseybert.com)

NAPKIN RINGS: Kim Seybert (kimseybert.com)

STEMWARE: Nachtmann (nachtmann.com)

FLATWARE: Mepra (theluxuryartmepra.com)

DERBY HAT DESIGNER: Rachelle Willnus, Derby Hats by Rachelle

MEN'S CLOTHING: Barakat Bespoke (barakatbespoke.com)

MENU CARDS: By Invitation Only (byinvitationonlylr.com)

CALLIGRAPHY: By Invitation Only (byinvitationonlylr.com)

HORSE: Red Hot Momma, Six-Time World Champion Show Horse

FOOD STYLIST: Muriel Wilkins

MODELS: Derrell Hartwick, Sarah Hutchinson Wengel, McKenzie Smith, Sidney Selakovich, Conley Harrison

SPECIAL THANKS: Bob Mullenax, Stacy Husman, Mary Thomas

Lewis, Herren Hickingbotham, Mario Garcia, Baldwin and Shell Construction Company, Sydnee Chun, Jana Claire Bishop, John Paul King, Carrie Kessler, Stacey Selakovich, Dale Aldridge, Tammy Copeland, Brittany Vick, Rachelle Willnus

Spring Rehearsal Dinner

EVENT DESIGN: Shayla Copas (shaylacopas.com)

PHOTOGRAPHER: Janet Warlick, Camera Work Photography (cameraworkphoto.com)

And Erica Payne, E. Marie Design and Photography

CULINARY CONTRIBUTOR: Chef Tim Morton, RH Catering

VENUE: Farm of Linda and Rush Harding

VENUE INTERIOR DESIGN: Cathy Pursell

FLORAL: Tipton and Hurst Floral (tiptonhurst.com)

MENU CARDS: By Invitation Only (byinvitationonlylr.com)

CALLIGRAPHY: By Invitation Only (byinvitationonlylr.com)

DINNERWARE RENTALS: Posh Couture Rentals (poshcouturerentals.com)

EVENT FURNITURE RENTALS: Hanks Event Rentals (hankseventrentals.com)

SPECIAL THANKS: Linda and Rush Harding, Cathy Pursell, Tim Morton, Payne Harding

Easter

EVENT DESIGN: Shayla Copas (shaylacopas.com)

PHOTOGRAPHER: Janet Warlick, Camera Work Photography (cameraworkphoto.com)

CULINARY CONTRIBUTOR: Chef Don Bingham, former Arkansas Governor's Mansion administrator

VENUE: Arkansas Governor's Mansion (arkansasgovernorsmansion.com)

VENUE INTERIOR DESIGN: Shayla Copas Interiors (Dining Room and Living Room) (shaylacopas.com)

FLORAL DESIGN: Tanarah Haynie, Lead Floral Design, Tanarah Luxe Floral (tanarahluxefloral.com)

MENU CARDS: By Invitation Only (byinvitationonlylr.com)

CALLIGRAPHY: By Invitation Only (byinvitationonlylr.com)

LINEN AND NAPKIN FABRIC: Thibaut (thibautdesign.com)

LINEN SEAMSTRESS: Callie Bullock, Draped and Tailored

BRUNCH GUESTS: First Lady Susan Hutchinson, Sarah Hutchinson Wengel, Carla Emanuel, Anne Preston, Francesca Tolson, Lauren Frederick, Cindy Baker, Carmen Portillo, Sarah Mauppin, Courtney Kajevaski

SPECIAL THANKS: Arkansas First Lady Susan Hutchinson, Chef Don Bingham, Chef Daniel R. R. Darrah, Arkansas Governor's Mansion Association Volunteers, Misty Phillips, Sarah Hutchinson Wengel

SPECIAL NOTE: Shayla Copas purchased all food for this chapter. No state funds were expended. No expense was incurred to taxpayers or the Governor's Mansion.

Cinco de Mayo

EVENT DESIGN: Shayla Copas (shaylacopas.com)

PHOTOGRAPHER: Janet Warlick, Camera Work Photography (cameraworkphoto.com)

CULINARY CONTRIBUTOR: Chef Scott Rains, Table 28 (theburgundyhotel.com)

VENUE: Home of Susan and Herren Hickingbotham

FLORAL: Dale Aldridge, Tammy Copeland, and Brittany Vick of Silks A Bloom (silks-a-bloom.com)

LINEN AND NAPKIN FABRIC: Thibaut (thibautdesign.com)

LINEN SEAMSTRESS: Callie Bullock, Draped and Tailored

CHARGERS: Kim Seybert (kimseybert.com)

NAPKIN RINGS: Kim Seybert (kimseybert.com)

STEMWARE: Kim Seybert (kimseybert.com)

FLATWARE: Mepra (theluxuryartmepra.com)

CANDLES: Xela Aroma (xelaaroma.com)

DINNERWARE: Skyros Designs (skyrosdesigns.com)

MENU CARDS: By Invitation Only (byinvitationonlylr.com)

CALLIGRAPHY: By Invitation Only (byinvitationonlylr.com)

EVENT FURNITURE RENTALS: Hanks Event Rentals (hankseventrentals.com)

FOOD STYLIST: Muriel Wilkins

DINNER GUESTS: Susan Hickingbotham, Herren Hickingbotham, Tiffany Robinson, Daniel Robinson, Katie Ryburn, Jason Ryburn, Dr. Leslie Dickinson, Bart Dickinson, Francesca Tolson, Sarah Hutchinson Wengel, Jeanne Gulledge, Oliver Aguilar

SPECIAL THANKS: Herren and Susan Hickingbotham, Stacey Selakovich, Cassidy Reeves, Janna Claire Bishop, Dale Aldridge, Tammy Copeland, Brittany Vick, Sarah Hutchinson Wengel

Seersucker Social

EVENT DESIGN: Shayla Copas, Shayla Copas Interiors (shaylacopas.com)

PHOTOGRAPHER: Janet Warlick, Camera Work Photography (cameraworkphoto.com)

CULINARY CONTRIBUTOR: Chef Janice Provost, Parigi Dallas (parigidallas.com)

VENUE: Home of Paul and Kathryn Johnston

VENUE INTERIOR DESIGN: Emily Johnston Larkin (ejinteriors. net) and Kathryn Johnston

FLORAL: Tanarah Haynie, Tanarah Luxe Floral (tanarahluxefloral.com)

MENU CARDS: By Invitation Only (byinvitationonlylr.com)

CALLIGRAPHY: By Invitation Only (byinvitationonlylr.com)

PLACECARDS: By Invitation Only (byinvitationonlylr.com)

FLATWARE: Kim Seybert (kimseybert.com)

NAPKIN RINGS: Kim Seybert (kimseybert.com)

PLACEMATS: Kim Seybert (kimseybert.com)

STEMWARE: Orrefors (orrefors.us)

LINEN AND NAPKIN FABRIC: Thibaut (thibautdesign.com)

LINEN SEAMSTRESS: Callie Bullock, Draped and Tailored

DINNER GUESTS: Sarah Polzer, Catherine Spavital, Andrew Gonzales, Oscar Gutierrez, Keitha Wright, Alejandro Gonzalez, Emily Larkin,

SPECIAL THANKS: Emily Johnston Larkin, Paul and Kathy Johnston, Oscar Gutierrez

Poolside Soiree

EVENT DESIGN: Shayla Copas (shaylacopas.com)

PHOTOGRAPHER: Janet Warlick, Camera Work Photography (cameraworkphoto.com)

CULINARY CONTRIBUTOR: Chef Tim Morton, RH Catering

VENUE: Home of Shayla and Scott Copas

VENUE INTERIOR DESIGN: Shayla Copas Interiors (shaylacopas.com)

FLORAL: Angie Strange, Posh Floral Designs (poshforal.com)

LINENS: BBJ Linen Rental (bbjlinen.com)

CALLIGRAPHY: By Invitation Only (byinvitationonlylr.com)

DINNER GUESTS: Donna and David Cone, Terri and Chuck Erwin, Druann and Barry Baskin, Lynn and George O'Connor, Vicki and Mark Saviers

Fourth of July

EVENT DESIGN: Shayla Copas (shaylacopas.com)

PHOTOGRAPHER: Janet Warlick, Camera Work Photography (cameraworkphoto.com)

CULINARY CONTRIBUTOR: Chef Scott Rains, Table 28 (theburgundyhotel.com)

VENUE: Home of Teresa and Dr. Joseph Murphy

FLORAL: Dale Aldridge, Tammy Copeland, and Brittany Vick of Silks A Bloom (silks-a-bloom.com)

STEMWARE: Riedel (riedel.com)

FLATWARE: Kim Seybert (kimseybert.com)

DINNERWARE: Skyros Designs (skyrosdesigns.com)

NAPKIN RINGS: Kim Seybert (kimseybert.com)

PLACEMATS: Kim Seybert (kimseybert.com)

LINEN AND NAPKIN FABRIC: Thibaut (thibautdesign.com)

LINEN SEAMSTRESS: Callie Bullock, Draped and Tailored

MENU CARDS: By Invitation Only (byinvitationonlylr.com)

CALLIGRAPHY: By Invitation Only (byinvitationonlylr.com)

EVENT FURNITURE RENTALS: Hanks Event Rentals (hankseventrentals.com)

FOOD STYLIST: Muriel Wilkins

DINNER GUESTS: Samantha Knoll, Drew Knoll, Anne-Claire Owens, Chris Owens, Sarah Hutchinson Wengel, Dave Wengel, Brooke Butler, Francesca Tolson, Oliver Aguilar, Lauren Frederick

SPECIAL THANKS: Teresa and Dr. Joseph Murphy, Janna Claire Bishop, Anne-Claire Owens, Stacey Selakovich, Mary Browne Allen, Dale Aldridge, Tammy Copeland, Brittany Vick

Under the Sea

EVENT DESIGN: Shayla Copas (shaylacopas.com)

PHOTOGRAPHER: Janet Warlick, Camera Work Photography (cameraworkphoto.com)

CULINARY CONTRIBUTOR: Chef Payne Harding, Cache Restaurant (cachelittlerock.com)

VENUE: Home of Shayla and Scott Copas

VENUE INTERIOR DESIGN: Shayla Copas Interiors (shaylacopas.com)

FLORAL DESIGN: Tanarah Haynie, Lead Floral Design, Tanarah Luxe Floral (tanarahluxefloral.com)

MENU CARDS: Carmen Portillo, Cocoa Belle Chocolates (cocobellechocolates.com)

CALLIGRAPHY: By Invitation Only (byinvitationonlylr.com)

NAPKINS: Kim Seybert (kimseybert.com)

NAPKIN RINGS: Kim Seybert (kimseybert.com)

PLACEMATS: Kim Seybert (kimseybert.com)

RUNNER: Kim Seybert (kimseyert.com)

SHELL CONTAINERS: John Richard

DINNER GUESTS: Aaron Perkins, Oliver Aguilar, Carole Smith, Marvin Maurras, Dr. Suzanne Yee, Bill Yee, Katrinka Shields, Callie Bullock, Jenanne Filat

SPECIAL THANKS: Aaron Perkins

Fall Fest

EVENT DESIGN: Shayla Copas (shaylacopas.com)

PHOTOGRAPHER: Janet Warlick, Camera Work Photography (cameraworkphoto.com)

CULINARY CONTRIBUTOR: Chef Jamie McAfee, Pine Bluff Country Club (pinebluffcc.com)

VENUE: Goodwin Manor

FLORAL DESIGN: Tanarah Haynie, Tanarah Luxe Floral (tanarahluxefloral.com)

MENU CARDS: By Invitation Only (byinvitationonlylr.com)

CALLIGRAPHY: By Invitation Only (byinvitationonlylr.com)

LINEN AND NAPKIN FABRIC: Thibaut (thibautdesign.com)

LINEN SEAMSTRESS: Callie Bullock, Draped and Tailored

DINNER GUESTS: Aaron Perkins, Francesca Tolson, Brooke Butler, Lauren Frederick, Sarah Mauppin, Derrell Hartwick, Alisha Curtis, Oliver Aguilar, Jennifer Bruce

SPECIAL THANKS: Andrea Goodwin, Aaron Perkins, Sarah Hutchinson Wengel

Elegant Cabin

EVENT DESIGN: Shayla Copas (shaylacopas.com)

PHOTOGRAPHER: Janet Warlick, Camera Work Photography (cameraworkphoto.com)

CULINARY CONTRIBUTOR: Chef Jamie McAfee, Pine Bluff Country Club (pinebluffcc.com)

VENUE: Split River, cabin of Sharri and Bill Jones (sissyslogcabin.com)

FLORAL DESIGN: Tanarah Haynie, Tanarah Luxe Floral (tanarahluxefloral.com)

MENU CARDS: By Invitation Only (byinvitationonlylr.com)

CALLIGRAPHY: By Invitation Only (byinvitationonlylr.com)

LINEN AND NAPKIN FABRIC: Thibaut (thibautdesign.com)

DINNERWARE: Skyros Designs (skyrosdesigns.com)

PLACEMATS: Kim Seybert (kimseybert.com)

LINEN SEAMSTRESS: Callie Bullock, Draped and Tailored

DINNER GUESTS: Bill Jones, Sharri Jones, Lynne Franks, Hayden Franks, Shayla Copas, Scott Copas

SPECIAL THANKS: Bill and Sharri Jones

Oktoberfest

EVENT DESIGN: Shayla Copas, Shayla Copas Interiors (shaylacopas.com)

PHOTOGRAPHER: Janet Warlick, Camera Work Photography (cameraworkphoto.com)

CULINARY CONTRIBUTOR: Shay and Brian Geyer, IBB Design (ibbdesign.com)

VENUE: Home of Shay and Brian Geyer

VENUE INTERIOR DESIGN: Shay Geyer (ibbdesign.com)

FLORAL: Tanarah Haynie, Tanarah Luxe Floral (tanarahluxefloral.com)

MENU CARDS: By Invitation Only (byinvitationonlylr.com)

CALLIGRAPHY: By Invitation Only (byinvitationonlylr.com)

DINNERWARE: Skyros Designs (skyrosdesigns.com)

FLATWARE: Mepra (theluxuryartmepra.com)

NAPKIN RINGS: Kim Seybert (kimseybert.com)

LINEN AND NAPKIN FABRIC: Thibaut (thibautdesign.com)

LINEN SEAMSTRESS: Callie Bullock, Draped and Tailored

STEMWARE: Orrefors (orrefors.us)

BRATWURSTS: Bavarian Meats (bavarianmeats.com)

ARTIFICIAL SUNFLOWER ARRANGEMENT BY BEER FLIGHT: The Botanical Mix (thebotanicalmix.com)

DINNER GUESTS: Shay Geyer, Brian Geyer, Jaime Kimble, Penny Mayfield, John Mayfield, Ginger Reyna, Edward Reyna, Kim Gleason, Sean Gleason, Betsy Devenny, Jay Devenny, David Glass

SPECIAL THANKS: Shay and Brian Geyer

Thanksgiving

EVENT DESIGN: Shayla Copas (shaylacopas.com)

PHOTOGRAPHER: Janet Warlick, Camera Work Photography (cameraworkphoto.com)

CULINARY CONTRIBUTOR: First Lady Susan Hutchinson, Executive Chef Daniel R. R. Darrah, Chef Don Bingham, former Arkansas Governor's Mansion administrator

VENUE: Arkansas Governor's Mansion

VENUE INTERIOR DESIGN: Shayla Copas Interiors (Dining Room and Living Room) (shaylacopas.com)

FLORAL DESIGN: Tanarah Haynie, Tanarah Luxe Floral (tanarahluxefloral.com)

MENU CARDS: By Invitation Only (byinvitationonlylr.com)

CALLIGRAPHY: By Invitation Only (byinvitationonlylr.com)

PLACEMATS: Kim Seybert (kimseybert.com)

LINEN AND NAPKIN FABRIC: Thibaut (thibautdesign.com)

LINEN SEAMSTRESS: Callie Bullock, Draped and Tailored

DINNER GUESTS: Arkansas First Lady Susan Hutchinson, Sarah Hutchinson Wengel, Carole Smith, Aaron Perkins, Brooke Butler, Sarah Mauppin, Susan Hickingbotham, Herren Hickingbotham, Misty Phillips, Bradley Phillips, Lauren Frederick

SPECIAL THANKS: Arkansas First Lady Susan Hutchinson, Chef Don Bingham, Executive Chef Daniel R. R. Darrah, Arkansas Governor's Mansion Association Volunteers, Misty Phillips, Sarah Hutchinson Wengel

SPECIAL NOTE: Shayla Copas purchased all food for this event. No state funds were expended. No expense was charged to taxpayers or the Governor's Mansion.

Christmas

EVENT DESIGN: Shayla Copas, Shayla Copas Interiors (shaylacopas.com)

PHOTOGRAPHER: Janet Warlick, Camera Work Photography (cameraworkphoto.com)

CULINARY CONTRIBUTOR: Shay and Brian Geyer, IBB Design (ibbdesign.com)

VENUE: Home of Shay and Brian Geyer

VENUE INTERIOR DESIGN: Shay Geyer (ibbdesign.com)

FLORAL: Tanarah Haynie, lead floral designer, Tanarah Luxe Floral (tanarahluxefloral.com)

CHARGERS: Sparkles Home (sparkleshome.com)

MENU CARDS: By Invitation Only (byinvitationonlylr.com)

CALLIGRAPHY: By Invitation Only (byinvitationonlylr.com)

GUEST GIFTS: IBB Design (ibbdesign.com)

DINNER GUESTS: Shay Geyer, Brian Geyer, Richard Reupke, Paige Reupke, Jaime Kimble, Penny Mayfield, John Mayfield, Ginger Reyna, Edward Reyna, Jeff Osbourne, Kim Osbourne

SPECIAL THANKS: Shay and Brian Geyer

New Year's Eve

EVENT DESIGN: Shayla Copas (shaylacopas.com)

PHOTOGRAPHER: Janet

Warlick, Camera Work Photography (cameraworkphoto.com)

CULINARY CONTRIBUTOR: Jim Norton, *The Norton Recipe*

VENUE: Home of Jim Norton and Robert Walden

VENUE INTERIOR DESIGN: Jim Norton and Robert Walden

FLORAL: Angie Strange, Posh Floral Designs (poshfloral.com)

PLACE MATS: Kim Seybert (kimseybert.com)

NAPKIN RINGS: Kim Seybert (kimseybert.com)

MENU CARDS: By Invitation Only (byinvitationonlylr.com)

CALLIGRAPHY: By Invitation Only (byinvitationonlylr.com)

LINEN AND NAPKIN FABRIC: Thibaut Pattern (thibautdesign.com)

LINEN SEAMSTRESS: Callie Bullock, Draped and Tailored

WINE: Robert Turner Wines (robertturnerwines.com)

DINNER GUESTS: Jim Norton, Robert Walden, Shayla Copas, Scott Copas, Patsy Camp, Chuck Freeman, Sherry Freeman, Amy Goodwin

SPECIAL THANKS: Jim Norton and Robert Walden

Valentine's

EVENT DESIGN: Shayla Copas (shaylacopas.com)

PHOTOGRAPHER: Janet Warlick, Camera Work Photography (cameraworkphoto.com)

CULINARY CONTRIBUTOR: Chef Payne Harding, Cache Restaurant (cachelittlerock.com)

VENUE: Home of Bill and Shirley Miller

VENUE INTERIOR DESIGN: Shayla Copas Interiors (shaylacopas.com)

FLORAL DESIGN: Tanarah Haynie, Tanarah Luxe Floral (tanarahluxefloral.com)

PLACEMATS: Kim Seybert (kimseybert.com)

NAPKIN RINGS: Kim Seybert (kimseybert.com)

MENU CARDS: By Invitation Only (byinvitationonlylr.com)

CALLIGRAPHY: By Invitation Only (byinvitationonlylr.com)

LINEN AND NAPKIN FABRIC: Thibaut (thibautdesign.com)

LINEN SEAMSTRESS: Callie Bullock, Draped and Tailored

DINNER GUESTS: Bill Miller, Shirley Miller, Scott Copas, Shayla Copas, Dr. Leslie Dickinson, Bart Dickinson, Tanarah Haynie, Rob Haynie

SPECIAL THANKS: Bill and Shirley Miller

Winter Wonderland

EVENT DESIGN: Shayla Copas (shaylacopas.com)

PHOTOGRAPHER: Janet Warlick, Camera Work Photography (cameraworkphoto.com)

CULINARY CONTRIBUTOR: Jim Norton, *The Norton Recipe*

VENUE: Home of Jim Norton and Robert Walden

VENUE INTERIOR DESIGN: Jim Norton and Robert Walden

FLORAL: Angie Strange, Posh Floral Designs (poshforal.com)

PLACEMATS: Kim Seybert (kimseybert.com)

NAPKIN RINGS: Kim Seybert (kimseybert.com)

MENU CARDS: By Invitation Only (byinvitationonlylr.com)

CALLIGRAPHY: By Invitation Only (byinvitationonlylr.com)

LINEN FABRIC: Thibaut (thibautdesign.com)

LINEN SEAMSTRESS: Callie Bullock, Draped and Tailored

WINE: Robert Turner Wines (robertturnerwines.com)

DINNER GUESTS: Robert Walden, Jim Norton, Dianne Norton, Onita Pellegrini, Loni Harris, Jimmy Harris, Mary Evelyn Pafford, Larry Pafford, Greg Alexander, Allycin Alexander

SPECIAL THANKS: Jim Norton and Robert Walden

Recipe Index

• • •

Salads

Side Dishes

Soups

Sauces and Glazes